# TAKE A WALK

## 100 Walks Through Natural Places in the Puget Sound Region

*Sue Muller Hacking*

SASQUATCH BOOKS

SEATTLE

*To my mother, Emily Muller O'Neill, for*
*believing in me, and to Clare Hodgson Meeker for her*
*encouragement and friendship. —S.M.H.*

Printed in the United States of America.
Distributed in Canada by Raincoast Books Ltd.

01          5 4

All photographs by the author

Art direction: Karen Schober
Cover and interior design and composition: Devorah Wolf
Maps: Devorah Wolf and Jennifer Harris
Copy editor: Alice Copp Smith

**Library of Congress Cataloging-in-Publication Data**
Hacking, Sue Muller.
   Take a walk : 100 walks through natural places in the Puget Sound region/
Muller Hacking.
      p.   cm.
   Includes bibliographical references (p. 212) and index.
   ISBN 1-57061-085-1
      1. Hiking—Washington (State)— Puget Sound Region—Guidebooks.
   2. Natural history—Washington (State)—Puget Sound Region—Guidebooks.
   3. Puget Sound Region (Wash.)—Guidebooks.  I. Title.
   GV199.42.W22P833  1997
   796.5'1'097977—dc21

                                                          96-51000
                                                          CIP

Sasquatch Books
615 Second Avenue, Suite 260
Seattle, Washington 98104
(206) 467-4300
books@sasquatchbooks.com
http://www.sasquatchbooks.com
Sasquatch Books publishes high-quality adult nonfiction and children's books
related to the Northwest (Alaska to San Francisco).
For more information about our titles, contact us at the address above,
or view our site on the World Wide Web.

# CONTENTS

## Acknowledgments

Many people have helped bring this project to reality. I could not have done it without the support and love of my family: Jon, Christopher, and Amanda, who put up with so much and walked so many miles. Special thanks go to Neil Strother, publisher of Northwest Prime Time Journal, for his belief in me as a writer and his good-humored editing of my "Nearby Trips" column, which became the genesis of this book. And many thanks go to all the great people at the city, county, and state parks who put up with my incessant questions and phone calls, and to Devorah Wolf for her design work. I especially appreciate my walk-loving friends who ventured forth with me, sometimes on a moment's notice: Clare Meeker, Stacy Young, Jagoda Perich-Anderson, Janette Wray, Janet Soares, Roshanak Clune and family, Chazz Hacking, Colin Hacking, Adrienne Ross, Angela McAuley, Brooke Thacker, Andy and Jan Dappen and daughters, Emily O'Neill, Chip Muller, Angela Ginorio, Emilia Muller-Ginorio, and Pamela Smith. Thanks to my colleagues-in-writing: Donna Bergman, Kathy Adler, and Clare Meeker, who had the patience to read rough drafts. And lastly, heartfelt thanks to Sarah Campbell and Gary Luke at Sasquatch Books for their encouragement and invaluable editorial comments.

# INTRODUCTION

WHEN I WAS YOUNGER, TAKING A WALK ALWAYS MEANT GOING TO THE mountains—either for multiday backpacking excursions or long day hikes. Now that I have children and all the errands of both working and running a household, I have less time, but I still have the same need for the tranquillity of a forest or beach.

Recently, I've turned more and more to the nearby urban and suburban parks. What glorious freedom, if only for an hour or two, to step from my car and immerse myself in the gentle pace of foot travel. It was the discovery of these small sanctuaries of nature—just a few minutes from home—and the lack of a concise guide that prompted me to begin work on this book.

Because of our mild Puget Sound climate, the walks described in this book are accessible year-round. In spring, the breezes through West Hylebos Wetlands State Park are pungent with the scent of newly opened skunk cabbage, and fluffy Canada goslings can be seen parading with their parents on the banks of Wapato Lake. In summer, sun-ripened blackberries cluster along Ellis Cove trail in Priest Point Park and on the low slopes of Cougar Mountain. As the days cool, the trail in Mercer Island's Pioneer Park rustles underfoot with fallen maple leaves, while migrating birds flock to the lakes and the Sound. And in winter, sword ferns on Lord Hill and grasses along the Sammamish River Trail dress in necklaces of white frost. No visit ever repeats itself. Like the mountains and the ocean, even these tiny green spaces in and around our cities offer ever-changing dramas of wildlife, plants, and weather.

## How These Walks Were Chosen

This book is designed to help you select easy, short walks just minutes from your home or workplace, be it in Olympia, Seattle, Everett, Issaquah, or any of the cities between. All walks in this book lie within a half-hour drive of a major urban center and all are on public land.

My criteria for a good walking trail are that it be at least 1 mile in length, surrounded by greenery or close to water, and that it allow no motorized vehicles. Most trails meet that minimum mile and others are part of a larger system of trails within a park where you are limited only by your energy and time. A few small parks, such as Schmitz Preserve,

Sunrise Beach Park, and Edith Moulton Park, may fall short on trail length but surpass others in beauty.

Most important was that the walks travel through natural places— everything from saltwater beaches and lakeshores to meadows and forests.

## Keeping Updated

As this book goes to press, park maintenance crews are paving old trails and creating new ones. More railroad right-of-ways are being acquired and converted to trails, and new nature preserves are in the works. Because of this constant growth and change, things may not be as I have portrayed them by the time you take some of these walks. With luck, the changes will be for the better.

## Thoughts on Safety

Not every trail is as safe as a suburban sidewalk. Despite maintenance efforts, nature often prevails. Mud slides obliterate paths, rain erodes them, and fallen trees block them. Walking in natural places can be risky. Wear appropriate footgear, and try to walk with someone else, especially in the more remote parks. Take common sense and anything else you need. You're on your own.

## Thoughts on Care and Preservation

I've had people beg me, on hearing that I was writing this book, not to reveal "their" special trail or park. One hiker told me, "We don't want a lot of city folks overrunning the trails, picking the flowers, not picking up after their dogs." Locals who care for their forests and wetlands don't want to see them destroyed by hordes of strangers from a neighboring town. I sympathize with their concerns but find their anger misdirected. After walking hundreds of miles in these urban sanctuaries, I've seen a lot of caring use and very little abuse.

When I do witness misuse of the trails, though, I speak up. I don't hesitate to tell people if they are where they shouldn't be with a dog or a bicycle. And while some people respond courteously, or retreat in embarrassment, I've often heard "Oh, I didn't know. I live right over there and come in here all the time." Proximity does not imply ownership or the right to abuse the forest. Sometimes the people who mistreat the trails and parks the most are the immediate neighbors, or their children, who feel that the nearby forests and natural spaces are personal playgrounds. Mountain bikers ride on trails that clearly say "Foot Traffic Only" and claim they never saw the sign. Children playing in "their" woods rip the moss from the nurse logs and let their dogs chase spawning salmon.

Happily, I've seen that most people who share the trails, whether they come from 5 or 50 minutes away, respect the natural areas and understand the need for preservation and care. When parents feel that way, they encourage the same feelings in their children. There is no "my park" or "your park." These are all *our* parks.

Whether parks are signposted or not, the same minimal courtesies are asked of all visitors:

1. Stay on the trail. As a Bellevue park sign says, "Plants grow by the inch, and die by the foot."

2. Keep pets on a leash unless in a designated off-leash area.

3. Keep children and pets out of salmon-spawning creeks.

4. Don't feed the waterfowl.

5. Take only pictures. Leave only footprints.

With everyone's cooperation, we can preserve our parks for ourselves and as a heritage for generations to come.

# HOW TO USE THIS BOOK

THE WALKS ARE ARRANGED ROUGHLY FROM NORTH TO SOUTH, GROUPED in chapters according to six urban hubs: Everett; Seattle (including Bainbridge Island); Bellevue (including Mercer Island); the cities of Des Moines, Renton, and Kent; Tacoma; and Olympia.

Each walk description includes:

**A quick location description** that places the walk very generally, in reference to an urban center. Distances given are in driving miles (not as the crow flies), from an approximation of the city's "downtown" area.

| | |
|---|---|
| HIGHLIGHTS | *The setting and other features that make this walk unique.* |
| TRAIL | *Approximate length in miles and type of surface (paved, gravel, or natural).* |
| OTHER USAGE | *Who shares the trail with you, the pedestrian (horses and/or bicycles). Although not noted, expect to share paved trails with skaters. None of these walks allow motorized vehicles. All allow pets on leash unless otherwise noted.* |
| STEEPNESS | *Level: Flat (or nearly so) Gentle: Easy ups and downs Moderate: Gets the heart rate up Steep: Stairs, or equivalent steepness* |
| CONNECTING TRAILS | *Trails that intersect the walk or are within a short walking distance.* |
| PARK SERVICES | *Restrooms (including freestanding facilities), picnic tables, interpretive walks, playing fields, playgrounds, etc. (Refer to maps and driving directions for parking information.)* |
| DISABLED ACCESS | *Americans with Disabilities Act (ADA) access, for the trail and/or park. Call the listed office for details: their definition of "accessible" and yours may differ.* |

Since the first printing of this book, area codes for the region have changed. The new area codes are listed in the References section on page 221.

**Walk descriptions** may include ecological, historical, and scenic information. They are not intended to be step-by-step trail guides; the hope is to entice and invite you to discover the pleasure of the walk on your own.

**Driving directions** from major interstates are included for each walk, under the assumption that drivers will also have a good road map with them in the car. *Take a Walk* directions are basic and brief; they will be of little help if you take a wrong turn. For bus connections, call your local transit authority. All parks listed are open daylight hours only unless otherwise noted. Park office phone numbers are listed at the end of the How to Get There section. Main numbers for parks departments are in the References section at the end of the book.

**Maps** are intended to give a general sense of the layout of the parks and trails. Do not rely on these maps to locate yourself in complex parks such as Bridle Trails, Cougar Mountain, Lord Hill, Tiger Mountain, Coal Creek, Seahurst, and other parks with extensive unofficial or unmaintained trails. Keep in mind that parks departments discourage use of these unofficial trails, also known as casual trails, due to erosion and potential hazards.

All maps are oriented with north as "up" and are not drawn to scale (refer to the listed trail length to gauge the size of the park). The difference between paved, gravel, and natural surface trails is not indicated due to constantly changing conditions.

*Map Legend*

- - - trail      ⋈ bridge

🅟 parking      ♠ forest

🆁 restrooms      ♥ orchard

⅋ picnic area      ∧ campgrounds

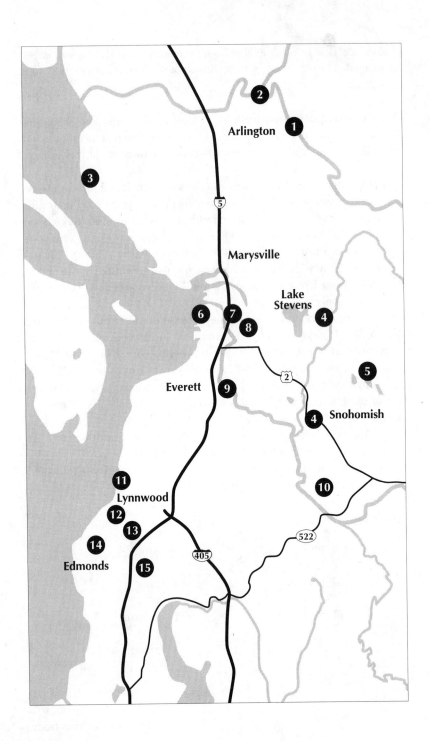

# IN AND AROUND EVERETT

# #1
# RIVER MEADOWS PARK

ARLINGTON, 20 MILES NORTH OF EVERETT

| | |
|---|---|
| HIGHLIGHTS | *River, forest, meadow* |
| TRAIL | *6.5 miles total; natural surface* |
| OTHER USAGE | *Bicycles* |
| STEEPNESS | *Level to moderate* |
| CONNECTING TRAILS | *None* |
| PARK SERVICES | *Restrooms, picnic shelter, campground, boat launch* |
| DISABLED ACCESS | *Restrooms* |

NESTLED ON THE BANKS OF THE STILLAGUAMISH, RIVER MEADOWS is both a working farm and a public park. Although the old barn is gone now and the orchard stands unpruned, the hay is harvested each year,

**Hay bales in River Meadows Park give the visitor a glimpse of farm life along the Stillaguamish**

and in summer rolled bales huddle on the browning field. In this rural setting, you may see coyote and deer, or eagles nesting along the river, or a red-tailed hawk soaring above.

Park near the Stillaguamish, where the air is fresh with the scent of river water. Walk north along the meadow edge, then enter the thickets of salal and blackberry that line the river beaches. Your feet are cushioned on sand and soft leaves as

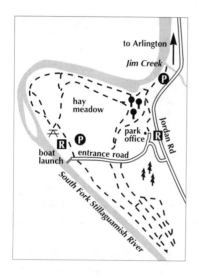

you walk under a canopy of cottonwoods and alders.

To the east, a small rise takes you up to the old orchard, where apple and pear trees blossom and later lure the deer from the forest for a nibble. North from the orchard you enter a lush alder and cedar forest on a dark, earthy path. The trail traverses a steep hillside with fine views to the river below.

If you go south from the orchard, across the entrance road, you enter a grove of ancient cedar stumps, from which you can climb uphill to a meadow or downhill back to the meadows by the river. In summer the trail by the river south of the parking lot may be densely lined with nettle and impassable with blackberry. In winter, the trails are clearer, and the sky is more visible under leafless alders covered in old man's beard and lichens.

**How to Get There:** From I-5 north of Everett, north- or southbound, take exit 208 (Arlington, SR 530). Go east on SR 530 4 miles to Arlington. Cross the Stillaguamish River bridge and go about 0.5 mile. Turn right on Arlington Heights Rd. After 1 mile turn right on Jordan Rd. Go 2 more miles to Jim Creek. There are two parking lots and trailheads here. The main park entrance is signposted on a white fence a few yards farther, also on the right. Snohomish County Parks (360) 435-3441.

# #2
# TWIN RIVERS PARK

ARLINGTON, 18 MILES NORTH OF EVERETT

| | |
|---|---|
| HIGHLIGHTS | *River, sandbars, meadows, Cascade views* |
| TRAIL | *0.5 mile riverfront, 1 mile total with loops and spurs; natural surface* |
| OTHER USAGE | *Bicycles* |
| STEEPNESS | *Level* |
| CONNECTING TRAILS | *None* |
| PARK SERVICES | *Restrooms, picnic tables, playing fields* |
| DISABLED ACCESS | *Restrooms* |

NESTLED IN THE CONFLUENCE OF THE NORTH AND SOUTH FORKS OF the Stillaguamish, this park on the edge of Arlington—and the brink of rural Washington—combines both active park amenities and the opportunity for riverside wandering.

From the northern parking lot, leave behind the calls and shouts of ball players, and enter the quiet of blackberry bushes and young alders. The air is rich with earth and water fragrance, and the paths are often defined more by the winter floods than by the impact of feet. A tangle of alder saplings leans awkwardly to the side, survivors of a marauding river. The hard-packed floodplain makes for easy walking. Wander along the banks of the South Fork, venturing out onto the expansive, round-pebbled beach. In summer, swallows

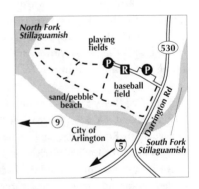

dive-bomb insects, and dippers bob on the water's edge. Among the berry bushes, cedar waxwings flit and squeal.

On the southern edge of the park along the South Fork, the forest is denser and cooler. The trails are soft dirt and brush-free. Here bigleaf maples present a splash of fall color, and in winter yield their leaves to the ground so that Cascade views are enhanced. You may also see harriers and hawks seeking supper in the meadows.

*How to Get There:* From I-5 north of Everett, north- or southbound, take exit 208 (Arlington, SR 530). Go east on SR 530 4 miles to Arlington. Cross the Stillaguamish River bridge. Turn left immediately into the park. Snohomish County Parks (360) 339-1208.

Bridges span the confluence of the North and South Forks of the Stillaguamish

# #3
# KAYAK POINT PARK

STANWOOD, ON PUGET SOUND, 17 MILES NORTH OF EVERETT

| | |
|---|---|
| HIGHLIGHTS | *Saltwater beach, bluff, forest, Olympic views* |
| TRAIL | *1.3 miles near beach; paved and natural surfaces* |
| OTHER USAGE | *Pedestrians only on forest trails; bicycles on paved trail* |
| STEEPNESS | *Level to steep* |
| CONNECTING TRAILS | *None* |
| PARK SERVICES | *Restrooms, picnic tables, shelters, year-round camping, fishing pier, brochure* |
| DISABLED ACCESS | *Restrooms, campground* |

FROM HIGH ON THE BLUFF YOU CAN SURVEY PUGET SOUND AND ITS ever-changing moods: wind and whitecaps, or slate-gray smooth. On calm summer days you can look down on the decks of passing boats. On cold blustery days you might silently cheer the windsurfers braving the frigid water. Bring your binoculars and watch for the bald eagles that nest on the hillside.

Kayak Point has a loosely defined set of trails, and because roads can take you quickly from bluff to beach, you have to choose to walk. Park near the ranger station and head into the campground on foot. Near Site 14 you'll find the start of the Eagle Scout trail, which snakes south and west past massive stumps and across a salal-filled forest floor beneath cedar and bigleaf maple. The trail closely follows the bluff line but, unless you have wandered too far east, is safely fenced. (Don't allow children to run ahead until you see the fencing.) Now the trail drops steeply, switching back on stairs and dirt to the southern end of the beach. Here, if it's a warm, sunny day, you leave the sylvan quiet and enter civilization with its unmistakable aroma of charcoal and grilling meat. Ahead of you stretches more than a mile of beach—sandy, log-strewn, and easy to walk. Explore the fishing pier to see who has caught what. Search the water below for jellyfish or the whiskered heads of harbor seals.

At the northern end of the beach, head inland to the base of the hill, where erosion has brought down giant trees and gouged the forest. You can choose either of two wooden staircases back to the ranger station to complete your loop.

*How to Get There:* From I-5 north of Everett, northbound, take exit 199 (Marysville, Tulalip). Turn left (west) on 4th St which becomes Tulalip Rd and then Marine View Dr. Go 13 miles and turn left into the park.

From I-5 north of Everett, southbound, take exit 206 (SR 531, Lakewood). Turn right (west) on Lakewood and go about 8 miles to Clarence Ave which becomes Marine View Dr. Turn left (south) and go about 2 miles to the park entrance. Snohomish County Parks (360) 652-7992.

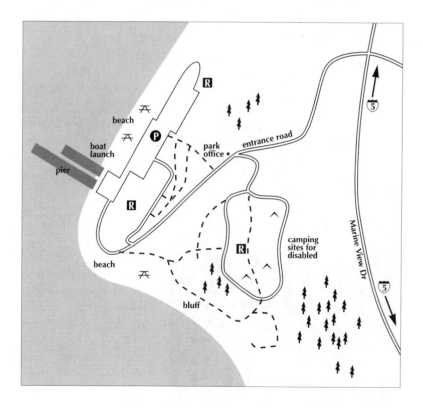

# #4
# CENTENNIAL TRAIL

LAKE STEVENS (8 MILES NORTHEAST OF EVERETT) TO
SNOHOMISH (8 MILES SOUTHEAST OF EVERETT)

| | |
|---|---|
| HIGHLIGHTS | *Farmland, mountain views, river* |
| TRAIL | *7.5 miles one way; paved rails-to-trails conversion* |
| OTHER USAGE | *Bicycles; horses in some sections* |
| STEEPNESS | *Level* |
| CONNECTING TRAILS | *None* |
| PARK SERVICES | *Restrooms, picnic tables* |
| DISABLED ACCESS | *Restrooms and trail access at both Pilchuck Trailhead on Machias Road and in Machias* |

JUST MINUTES EAST OF THE I-5 CORRIDOR LIES THE FERTILE SNOHOMISH Valley with its pastures, dairy farms, and picturesque barns. You've probably driven through it countless times en route to the Cascades or Eastern Washington. Now, the Centennial Trail lets you slow the pace and walk this valley, breathing the clear, fresh air (and, yes, sometimes the aroma of fertilizer). Views are expansive from the dairy-farm pastures to the peaks of the Cascades.

**The Centennial Trail passes by dairy farms in the fertile Snohomish Valley**

Like other paved, converted railroad grades, this trail is great for distance walking, stroller pushing, or bicycling. There are several trailheads, so you can choose to walk either north or south.

From historic downtown Snohomish, the trail parallels Maple

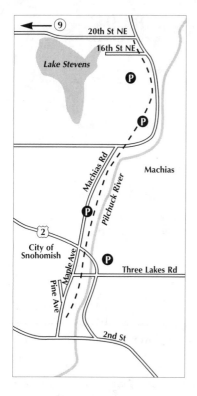

Street and the Pilchuck River. Soon, vistas open to embrace the pastures and farms. In the 1880s the settlers cleared trees and drained the swampy land to leave rich, fertile soil. Now, as then, it is prime dairy land. Cows and horses graze in the lush fields.

Just a few miles south of Lake Stevens, you pass the small town of Machias, where a replica of the old railroad station now serves as a rest area. Near its northern end, on the outskirts of Lake Stevens, the trail crosses several country roads and driveways, so be sure to keep kids in close check.

*How to Get There:* To reach the southern end (Snohomish): From I-5 in Everett, north- or southbound, take exit 194 (US 2 east, Wenatchee). Head east on US 2, bearing right (south) at the end of the trestle. Go about 2.5 miles to SR 9. Head south on SR 9 to the Snohomish/Riverview Rd/2nd St exit. Turn left on 2nd St. Go about 12 blocks and turn left (north) on Maple Ave. Park at the junction of Maple Ave and Pine Ave. More parking is found 1.5 miles north on Maple Ave (it becomes Machias Rd) at the Pilchuck Trailhead, just south of the US 2 underpass.

For the northern end (Lake Stevens): From I-5 in Everett, north- or southbound, take exit 194 (US 2, Wenatchee). Head east on US 2 bearing left (north) at the end of the trestle onto SR 204. Go 2.3 miles, following signs to Lake Stevens. Turn left (north) on SR 9, then right (east) on Lundeen Park Way. Shortly after passing Lundeen City Park, bear right on Vernon Rd which becomes N Lakeshore Dr. Turn right on 124th Ave NE, then left on 16th St NE. Park at the Bonneville Ball Fields. Snohomish County Parks (360) 568-8434.

# #5
# FLOWING LAKE PARK

**19 MILES EAST OF EVERETT**

| | |
|---:|:---|
| HIGHLIGHTS | *Forest, lakeshore* |
| TRAIL | *1-mile loop, including spurs and lakeside; natural surface* |
| OTHER USAGE | *Pedestrians only* |
| STEEPNESS | *Level to gentle* |
| CONNECTING TRAILS | *Local horse trail (difficult for walkers)* |
| PARK SERVICES | *Restrooms, playgrounds, picnic area, swimming, fishing, camping, boating* |
| DISABLED ACCESS | *Restrooms, campground* |

AWAY FROM THE BUSTLE OF PLAYGROUNDS AND BEACH, WALK THIS FOREST near the Cascade foothills, in which you can clearly see succession—the natural process of plants and animals taking over and replacing one an-

other as the forest ages. It was first logged a century ago, and those ancient stumps remain, or are broken down now to form nurse logs and stumps for younger trees. After two other loggings 60 and 40 years ago, cottonwoods and alders grew. But these trees are maturing now, giving way to new growth of cedar and fir, the trees of the original forest.

Some nurse logs are barely discernible under the mature trees towering out of them. Ancient snags still stand, homes to tiny creatures that provide meals for sapsuckers and woodpeckers.

The trail itself is natural-surface, soft underfoot. Forming a cir-

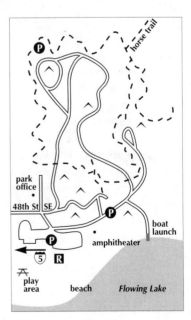

cle around the camps, it is unmarked but always returns you to the campground. Old wooden walkways lead over boggy areas. Near one of them you can try out "Fat Man's Squeeze," as it is dubbed by the rangers. This massive stump rises from the forest floor like a chimney,

its interior charred by the slash fire set by loggers a century ago. Crawling, you may just squeeze in—or maybe not. Like a rabbit in an open-topped warren, you can look up 20 feet to the circle of sky and branches above.

To complete a loop, follow the borders of the park out to the lake edge. Here, people-watching is fun, too, and walking the peri-meter of the park along the beach adds dis-tance to the walk.

Get a rabbit's-eye view of sky and forest from inside this old stump at Flowing Lake Park

*How to Get There:* From I-5 in Everett, north- or southbound, take exit 194 (US 2, Wenatchee). Head east on US 2, bearing right (south) at the end of the tres-tle. At milepost 10 turn left on 100th St SE (Westwick Rd). Go 2 miles to the French Creek Grange where the road bears sharply left (north) and becomes 171st Ave SE. Go 3 miles after the sharp bend and turn right on 48th St SE to the park entrance at the end of the road. Snohomish County Parks (425) 339-1208.

# #6
# JETTY ISLAND

EVERETT, 1.5 MILES FROM DOWNTOWN

| | |
|---|---|
| HIGHLIGHTS | *Salt marsh, dunes, beach, bird-watching* |
| TRAIL | *2–4 miles total, depending on tide; natural surface* |
| OTHER USAGE | *Pedestrians only; no pets* |
| STEEPNESS | *Level* |
| CONNECTING TRAILS | *None* |
| PARK SERVICES | *Free ferry mid-July to Labor Day; restrooms, picnic tables, guided interpretive walks, classes available summer only; no services from September to mid-July, though the park is open for those with boats* |
| DISABLED ACCESS | *None* |

BUILT ALMOST A HUNDRED YEARS AGO AT THE MOUTH OF THE SNOHOMISH River to create a freshwater harbor in Puget Sound, this manmade island has succeeded in ways its creators probably never imagined.

A southerly breeze cools the western shore and carries the scent of seaweed and the barks of the California sea lions. Sandpipers sprint on the mud flats, and ospreys soar above. Around the Scotch broom, swallows dart and dive for their insect meals and near the shore crabs scurry for shelter under rocks. In the salt marsh, salt crystals glisten on the stems of the pickleweed.

Measuring 2 miles long and a half mile wide, this wildlife preserve just three min-

**Seaweed and driftwood line Jetty Island**

utes from the Everett marina is the city's summer pride. Wednesday through Sunday for seven or eight weeks each summer, the 80-passenger ferry run by the Mosquito Fleet fills to capacity to take families, walkers, and bird lovers across the Snohomish River channel to the dock on Jetty Island. From there they disperse, though the majority cluster around the picnic tables on the western shore. To find solitude, walk either north or south for three or four minutes. You'll think you're on a deserted island—just you, the terns, herons, swallows, and the shimmering, slippery, pungent sea lettuce that lines the beach.

At low tide you can circumnavigate the island on the mud flats, though you have to be willing to get your feet squishy with mud. On the western side, a berm built by the Army Corps of Engineers has created a new salt marsh. It is here you are likely to see many of the more than 40 species of birds that visit or nest on the island. In early summer, expect to be divebombed by protective mother gulls warning you away from their nests.

*How to Get There:* From I-5 in Everett, northbound, take the left exit 192 (Broadway, Naval Station). Head north on Broadway. Go about 1.4 miles and turn left (west) on Everett Ave. Go over the hill through town to W. Marine View Dr. Turn right (north) and go 1.75 miles. Turn left (west) at 10th St into 10th St Boat Launch and Marine Park.

From I-5 in Everett, southbound, take exit 194 (SR 2, Wenatchee, Everett Ave). Turn right (west) on Everett Ave and go over the hill through town to W Marine View Dr. Turn right (north) and proceed as above. Everett Parks, July–August: (206) 257-8304; September–June: (206) 257-8300.

# 7

# LANGUS RIVERFRONT PARK

### EVERETT, 6 MILES EAST OF DOWNTOWN

| | |
|---|---|
| HIGHLIGHTS | *Cascade views, river* |
| TRAIL | *3-mile loop; paved and gravel* |
| OTHER USAGE | *Bicycles* |
| STEEPNESS | *Level* |
| CONNECTING TRAILS | *Spencer Island (Walk #8): no bicycles or pets allowed* |
| PARK SERVICES | *Restrooms, picnic tables, boat launch* |
| DISABLED ACCESS | *Restrooms, picnic area, trail* |

OLD BARGES DOCKED FOREVER AGAINST THE BANK OF THE SMOOTH-flowing Snohomish River recall days gone by when rivers and lakes, not roads, united the Northwest. Well-tended lawns and a paved walkway seem so genteel compared to the stalwart pilings of old docks. Great blue herons and belted kingfishers feed from the river—one on foot, the other on the wing—and migrating waterfowl rest in the reeds along the shore.

Langus Riverfront Park can be enjoyed with a civilized promenade along the riverfront—a hefty mile round trip, if you park at the northern end—or with a 3-mile triangular loop walk along the Snohomish River and the Union Slough. For the longer loop, continue south after the pavement ends, passing under the imposing I-5 freeway bridge. The first stretch follows the river, on which fishing boats, tugs, tourist boats, and an occasional log boom float by. At the southernmost point, Picnic Point, views open to grasslands and the Cascades and, on clear days, Mount Rainier.

**Petering Out?** *Keep energy up with water and snacks. Reward kids for reaching landmarks like hilltops or streams. Tell them how far they've walked (in miles!) and congratulate them.*

Along Union Slough a variety of deciduous trees line the pathway on a dike above the tidal trough. Across the water (if it's high tide) or mud (if it's low tide) lie the marshes, ponds, and dikes of Spencer Island (Walk #8). Jackknife Bridge ahead spans Union Slough and serves as an entrance to the preserve. From there, retrace your route to stay on pavement, or complete the loop by walking the maintenance road (South 4th Street) back to the river. Here you walk between the waste treatment ponds, where waterfowl abound. With binoculars you can see a palette of colors: the distinct black and white plumage of the hooded merganser, the orange bill of the scoter, or the blue bill of the male ruddy duck in late spring.

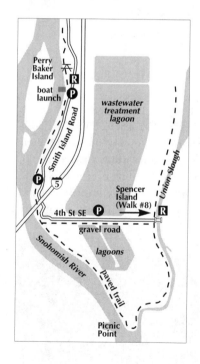

*How to Get There:* **From I-5 in Everett, northbound, take exit 195 (Port of Everett, Marine View Dr). Turn left, then merge to the right onto SR 529 north (Pacific Hwy). After crossing the Snohomish River take the first road to the right (signposted Smith Island Rd) and follow it (staying right) to the park.**

**From I-5 north of Everett, southbound, take exit 198 (SR 529 south, N Broadway). Go south on N Broadway (SR 529) over two bridges. Look for a brown sign for Langus Riverfront Park, and turn right onto the frontage road. Follow the road left under 529 and at another sign for the park turn right. Stay to the right for Smith Island Rd which leads to the park. Everett Parks (206) 257-8300.**

# #8
# SPENCER ISLAND

EVERETT, 6.5 MILES EAST OF DOWNTOWN

| | |
|---|---|
| HIGHLIGHTS | *Estuary, wetlands, nature preserve, bird-watching* |
| TRAIL | *3.5-mile loops, 0.5 mile cross-trail; natural surface* |
| OTHER USAGE | *Pedestrians only; no pets* |
| STEEPNESS | *Level* |
| CONNECTING TRAILS | *Langus Riverfront Park (Walk #7)* |
| PARK SERVICES | *Restrooms, bike rack near footbridge* |
| DISABLED ACCESS | *None* |

NEWLY CREATED SPENCER ISLAND IS A BIRDER'S PARADISE, AND A FREQUENT destination for Audubon Society field trips. On bright days the ruddy ducks and American widgeons appear to be floating on top of their upside-down twins as they waft across the mirrorlike surface of the pond. Northern harriers and red-tailed hawks hunt overhead. In the still waters by the marsh grasses, you might see river otters flipping and diving for fish. Nesting boxes for wood ducks and swallows dot numerous islands in the marsh, and on the southern loop bat boxes make welcome homes for these flying mammals.

But even without binoculars and a passion for birds, the miles of trail along dikes above the estuary are inviting for their hours of strolling and scenery-gazing. After entering the preserve over Jackknife Bridge, turn either north or south on the wide, wood chip–lined paths that form the northern and southern loops. To the east, Mount

**From farmland to nature preserve: Spencer Island**

Pilchuck dominates the skyline, and to the north, Mount Baker stands clear and proud.

Early settlers created dikes and sloughs to remove the tidal influx of salt water and to protect their farmlands. When Washington State, Snohomish County, and the City of Everett joined forces in the early 1990s to return this area to its natural state, they breached the dike wall with culverts and bridges. Now the wetland is an estuary again, responding to the ebb and flow of the tides from Puget Sound. This combination of fresh water and salt water provides a habitat for hundreds of species of birds and mammals.

From mid-October to mid-January the northern loop (administered by the Department of Fish and Wildlife) is open to hunting, so most walkers go south during those months. Interpretive signs give both history and natural history information. Benches and viewing platforms add a human touch to this otherwise wild and beautiful estuary.

*How to Get There:* From I-5 in Everett, northbound, take exit 195 (Port of Everett, Marine View Dr). Turn left and follow the road as it curves, eventually turning right onto Walnut St which becomes SR 529 north (Pacific Hwy). After crossing the Snohomish River take the first road to the right (signposted Smith Island Rd) and follow it (staying right) through Langus Riverfront Park. Park at the southern end of Langus (near the I-5 overpass) and walk east on 4th St SE to the Jackknife Bridge which leads to Spencer Island.

From I-5 north of Everett, southbound, take exit 198 (SR 529 south, N Broadway). Go south on N Broadway (SR 529) and turn right onto the frontage road. Follow the road left under 529 and at another sign for Spencer Island turn right. Stay to the right for Smith Island Rd which leads to Langus Riverfront Park. Proceed as above. Snohomish County Parks (425) 339-1208.

# #9
# LOWELL RIVERFRONT TRAIL

**EVERETT, 2.5 MILES SOUTHEAST OF DOWNTOWN**

| | |
|---|---|
| HIGHLIGHTS | *River, wetlands, meadow, Cascade views, bird-watching* |
| TRAIL | *1.6 miles one way; paved* |
| OTHER USAGE | *Bicycles* |
| STEEPNESS | *Level* |
| CONNECTING TRAILS | *None* |
| PARK SERVICES | *Restrooms, picnic tables* |
| DISABLED ACCESS | *Restrooms and trail* |

THIS STRIP OF MANICURED TRAIL ON THE BANKS OF THE SNOHOMISH River offers intimate river-edge walking and dramatic views of the Cascades. A late-afternoon visit reveals the Cascades set in bright relief to the east and a sheen of slate blue and mauve on the glassy Snohomish River. In contrast to the manicured park, the river is lined with old tumbledown shacks and craggy remains of piers. Pilings bound by cable still stand, resisting the unrelenting push of the water.

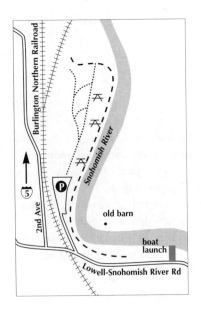

A bustling private industrial site for the past century, this area is now being restored to its natural state of meadow and wetland. From the parking lot, head either north or south. The walk to the south is more sylvan, with cottonwoods, alders, and blackberry thickets by the river. Across the water a barn, now softened by weathering, winds, and climbing vines, squats on its old foundation. It was here that E. D. Smith ran a sawmill and a logging camp, with a store, a post office, and a blacksmith shop, from the 1860s to the 1880s. For decades, the river was active with boats and log barges making their way to the Everett mills.

If you walk north from the parking lot you'll find a more parklike setting, with lawns, benches, and picnic tables. When the trail turns west into a sandy meadow, you can loop back to the parking lot on one of the myriad casual trails or return on the pavement by the river's edge.

Walk from end to end and you'll have covered more than 3 miles, perhaps still wishing for more.

*How to Get There:* From I-5 in Everett, northbound, take the left lane exit 192 (Broadway, Naval Station). Stay in the right-hand lane. Go under two overpasses. Take the cloverleaf to the right to 41st St. (This merges with the southbound exit from I-5 at 41st St.) At the stop sign on 41st St turn left (east). Stay in the right-hand lane to go over the freeway. Turn right immediately on Junction Ave. Go 6 or 7 blocks. Bear left on 47th St SE, then right onto S 2nd Ave. At the 4-way stop at Lenora, turn left on Lowell–Snohomish River Rd. The park is on the left just past the railroad tracks.

From I-5 in Everett, southbound, take exit 192 (41st St, Evergreen Way). Turn left (east) on 41st St over the freeway. Go right (south) on Junction Ave and proceed as above. Everett Parks (206) 257-8300.

Walkers pause for a moment along historic Snohomish River

# #10
# LORD HILL REGIONAL PARK

### 15 MILES SOUTHEAST OF EVERETT

| | |
|---:|:---|
| HIGHLIGHTS | *Forest, ponds, wetlands, Cascade and Olympic views* |
| TRAIL | *17 miles total; gravel and natural surfaces* |
| OTHER USAGE | *Bicycles, horses* |
| STEEPNESS | *Gentle to moderate* |
| CONNECTING TRAILS | *None* |
| PARK SERVICES | *Restrooms* |
| DISABLED ACCESS | *None* |

IN THE MIDDLE OF THE SNOHOMISH RIVER VALLEY, A SINGLE HILL RISES 600 feet above the floodplain, welcoming walkers and horses to its wild and shaded forest paths. A remnant of long-ago volcanic outcroppings, Lord Hill derives its name from homesteader Mitchell Lord, who dairy-

The Pipeline Trail cuts a swath of meadow through the forest in Lord Hill Park

farmed the flat land below the hill in the 1880s. By the 1930s the last old-growth timber had been cut, and in the 1980s the Department of Natural Resources cut patches of second-growth forest, producing today's multi-aged forest/wetland habitat.

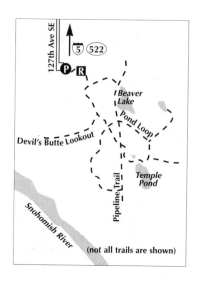

(not all trails are shown)

From the parking lot, head down the fragrant wood-chip path deep into the fir, hemlock, and maple forest. Where the trail levels, you'll be glad of sturdy puncheon bridges that span the miniature wetlands along the horse-trodden trail.

Soon the wood chips and puncheons give way to a wide, graveled path, leading to a T junction. To the left you reach one of the park's nine ponds. Turning right takes you up a rise in dense forest from which several trails branch off.

The map at the parking lot can be confusing and until the signage and trails are completed, keep your internal compass working and ask equestrians the way out if you're not sure. With luck, you'll find more ponds (one with active beavers), a cleared power-line trail, and viewpoints of Mount Baker to the north and the Olympics to the west.

**How to Get There:** From I-5 in Everett, north- or southbound, take exit 194 (US 2, Wenatchee). Head east on US 2, bearing south at the end of the trestle. Go about 2.5 miles to SR 9 and turn right (south). At the Snohomish/Riverview Rd/2nd St exit, turn left on 2nd St, then right onto Lincoln Ave S (which becomes the Old Snohomish-Monroe Hwy). Go 2.7 miles and turn right (south) on 127th Ave SE. Go 2 miles to 150th St SE. Turn left into the parking lot. Snohomish County Parks (206) 339-1208.

# #11
# MEADOWDALE BEACH PARK

LYNNWOOD, ON PUGET SOUND, 14.5 MILES SOUTHWEST OF EVERETT

| | |
|---|---|
| HIGHLIGHTS | *Forested ravine, stream, saltwater beach* |
| TRAIL | *2.5-mile round trip; paved (in lower meadow) and natural surfaces* |
| OTHER USAGE | *Bicycles* |
| STEEPNESS | *Moderate to steep* |
| CONNECTING TRAILS | *None* |
| PARK SERVICES | *Restrooms, picnic tables* |
| DISABLED ACCESS | *Restrooms, picnic area, paved trail; call (206) 339-1208 to request disabled parking pass to beach and picnic area* |

A GRACEFULLY CURVED DESCENT ON A WIDE, GRAVELED TRAIL BRINGS you into the aromatic forest. By keeping your eyes low on the huge bases of the Douglas fir and cedar stumps, you can envision these giants as they were a hundred years ago before they were cut for the mills. Robins and rufous-sided towhees hop slowly from the trail.

This upland-to-beach park was created with walkers in mind. Although the beach is car-accessible to those who need to drive, the layout forces all others to take the one-and-a-quarter-mile walk from the upper parking lot to the beach.

Small mileposts help you keep track of the distance traveled. At half a mile a washout shows the power of water and the need to preserve soil-retaining plants on steep hillsides. Beside the trail, Lund's Gulch Creek cuts a swath in the forest and whispers its wet

**Seashells in the Forest?** *Chances are these shells were brought not by children but by birds. Northwest crows and gulls have learned that the easiest way to open their shellfish meals is to let gravity and impact do the work. They pick up a shell from the beach, fly high, and drop it— repeatedly—until lunch is laid out for them. Oysters on the half shell, anyone?*

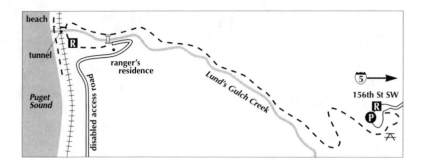

sounds on its way to Puget Sound. At the footbridge, you can choose to cross to the picnic area, lawns, and lower parking lot, or continue straight, still in the woods, to arrive at the tunnel to the beach. You may hear a train whistle blow, then watch a long freight chug past on the tracks that separate the forest from the sand.

To reach the water, pass beneath the tracks in the echo-filled tunnel. After the narrow ravine, the view feels exceptionally expansive. The snowy, hazy forms of the Olympics rise in the west, ferries from Mukilteo and Edmonds ply the Sound, and at low tide the beach beckons you to explore its rippled sand.

*How to Get There:* **From I-5 south of Everett, north- or southbound, take exit 183 (164th St SW). Turn west (right if southbound, left if northbound) on 164th St SW and go 1.7 miles to the intersection of 168th St SW and SR 99. Cross SR 99 and continue west. Go 2 blocks and turn right on 52nd Ave W. Turn left on 160th St SW, then right onto 56th Ave W. Turn left onto 156th St SW to the park entrance at the end of the road. Allow walking time (about 30 minutes) to return to the parking lot from the beach in daylight. Snohomish County Parks (206) 745-5111.**

# #12
# LYNNDALE PARK

### LYNNWOOD, 15 MILES SOUTHWEST OF EVERETT

| | |
|---|---|
| HIGHLIGHTS | *Forest* |
| TRAIL | *1.5 miles total; paved and natural surfaces* |
| OTHER USAGE | *Bicycles on paved trails* |
| STEEPNESS | *Level to steep* |
| CONNECTING TRAILS | *None* |
| PARK SERVICES | *Restrooms, picnic shelter, playground, sports courts, amphitheater* |
| DISABLED ACCESS | *Restrooms, picnic shelter, paved trail* |

LIKE MANY OTHER NEIGHBORHOOD PARKS, THIS ONE HIDES ITS BEST features behind sports courts and picnic shelters. Very accessible to wheelchairs, strollers, and little feet in skates, a generous half-mile paved trail leads from the parking lots, past an amphitheater, and into quiet second-growth forest. Here bigleaf maples form a cool canopy in summer or create graceful frames around a pale winter sky. Autumn paints the forest orange, red, yellow, and brown.

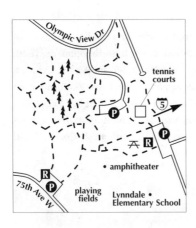

The paved trail crosses wide gravel trails and narrow natural trails, all hinting at the possibilities for exploration. Venture onto the natural trails and find the ravine (an old gravel pit, long ago reclaimed by nature) and the new wooden steps, the latter courtesy of the local Boy Scouts. The park boundaries are clear, so wander at will.

***How to Get There:*** From I-5 south of Everett, northbound, take exit 181 (SR 524, Lynnwood, 44th Ave W). Turn left (north) on 44th Ave W and go under the freeway. Go 2 blocks and turn left onto 196th St SW. Go about 2.5 miles and turn right (north) on 68th Ave W at the light. Turn left on 189th Pl SW to reach the parking lot.

From I-5 south of Everett, southbound, take exit 181 (SR 524, Lynnwood). Turn right (west) on 196th St SW. Go about 2.2 miles and turn right (north) on 68th Ave W at the light. Proceed as above. Lynnwood Parks (206) 771-4030.

Bigleaf maples at Lynndale Park tower overhead

# #13
# SCRIBER LAKE PARK

**LYNNWOOD, 15 MILES SOUTHWEST OF EVERETT**

| | |
|---|---|
| HIGHLIGHTS | *Wetlands, peat bog, bird-watching, art* |
| TRAIL | *1.5-mile loop and spurs; paved and natural surfaces* |
| OTHER USAGE | *Bicycles, except on soft-surface trails, where they are discouraged* |
| STEEPNESS | *Level* |
| CONNECTING TRAILS | *Scriber Creek Trail and Lynnwood–Everett Interurban* |
| PARK SERVICES | *Restrooms, picnic tables, playground* |
| DISABLED ACCESS | *Restrooms, paved trail* |

THIS LUSH POCKET OF WETLANDS BEAUTY IS SO CENTRAL TO DOWNTOWN Lynnwood that it was proposed as the site of the Civic Center in the 1960s. Luckily, sanity prevailed, leaving this magical landscape of stream, ponds, peat bogs, and wildlife undisturbed.

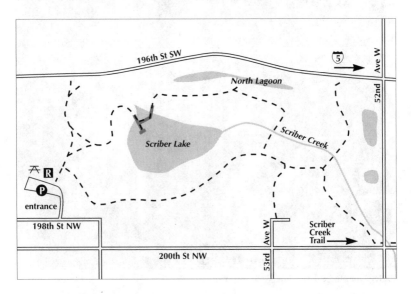

Follow a bark-chip trail across the top of 50-foot-deep peat, where yellow iris, Labrador tea, and cattails harbor salamanders, frogs, migrant waterfowl, and nesting birds. Interpretive signs explain the vital role of the marsh in purifying water and providing essential habitat to Northwest species. Side trails lead to homes or other small parks. From the paved trail on the south side of the lake, follow the short, steep natural trail to the south to see a strange example of a western red cedar—19 trunks rising from a central core like a giant candelabra. Follow the stream trail to 200th Street SW, turn left, and after a block of sidewalk cross Cedar Valley Road. There, enter another sliver of the park with pond and wetland. A footpath leads all the way to the Park and Ride near I-5.

*Art Along the Trails: Public art works along these trails range in sophistication and variety from Native American carving to children's mosaics, from the* **Sound Garden** *to wrought iron bench backs. These projects add variety and interest to the walks. Have you found the park with totem poles? Cast figures? Mosaics? How about an earth sculpture?*

When wet weather or winter storms flood the chipped path, stick to the paved walkway on the south side of the lake. Even in dry weather, though, the lake may rise above portions of the walkway. That's due to a family of beavers who have their own ideas about how to use the water in Scriber Lake.

*How to Get There:* **From I-5 south of Everett, northbound, take exit 181 (SR 524, Lynnwood, 44th Ave W). Turn left (north) on 44th Ave W and go under the freeway. Go 2 blocks and turn left onto 196th St SW. Go about 1 mile and turn left on Scriber Lake Rd (across from 58th Ave W). Take the first left on 198th St SW. Park entrance is on the left.**

**From I-5 south of Everett, southbound, take exit 181 (SR 524, Lynnwood). Turn right (west) on 196th St SW. Go about 1.5 miles and turn left on Scriber Lake Rd (across from 58th Ave W). Proceed as above. Lynnwood Parks (206) 771-4030.**

# #14
# YOST PARK

EDMONDS, 17 MILES SOUTHWEST OF EVERETT

| | |
|---|---|
| HIGHLIGHTS | *Forested ravine, wetlands, stream* |
| TRAIL | *About 1 mile total; natural surface* |
| OTHER USAGE | *Pedestrians only* |
| STEEPNESS | *Gentle to steep* |
| CONNECTING TRAILS | *None* |
| PARK SERVICES | *Restrooms, picnic tables, playground, swimming pool, interpretive trail map* |
| DISABLED ACCESS | *Restrooms, pool area, Ridge Trail* |

DESPITE ITS WELL-TRODDEN TRAILS, THIS RAVINE OF WOODED WILDNESS in a neat residential area of Edmonds may be unknown to folks who come for the more obvious pleasures: swimming and picnicking. Deep in the greenery below the pool, Shell Creek cuts a path through a mature forest of Douglas fir and maple.

To walk in this sylvan wonderland, leave the parking lot by the yellow maintenance gate and stroll Ridge Trail (the paved maintenance road) along the rim of the gulch. From here you can look into the upper branches of maples and firs as though you were an owl perched nearby, surveying all your domain. Descend the natural trail, letting the shouts of playing children fade above you. Listen instead for the high tinkling warble of the winter wren or the *dee-dee-dee* of the black-capped chickadee.

Wooden bridges and walkways cross Shell Creek and its tributaries (some dry by late summer). The eroded banks of these streams show evidence of winter flooding. Old stumps, long dead themselves, now provide life to saplings of cedar and elderberry. A loop trail encircles the base of the ravine, then climbs again to rejoin the rim trail. Other feeder trails branch off, some rising steeply up the hillside and then petering out, others emerging on Main Street to the north. Numbered posts correspond to notes on an informal nature guide that is available at the pool or the city parks office. To the west, the trail ends at the remains of an old concrete dam.

*How to Get There:* From I-5 south of Everett, northbound, take exit 177 (SR 104, Edmonds). Turn left and go under the freeway. Go about 2.8 miles and turn right on 100th Ave W. Go about 1 mile and turn right on Walnut St (which becomes Bowdoin Way). The park is on the corner of Bowdoin Way and 96th Ave W.

From I-5 south of Everett, southbound, take exit 181 (SR 524, Lynnwood). Turn right on 196th St SW. Go about 4.25 miles and turn left on 9th Ave S. Go 1 mile, turn left on Walnut and proceed as above. Edmonds Parks (206) 771-0230.

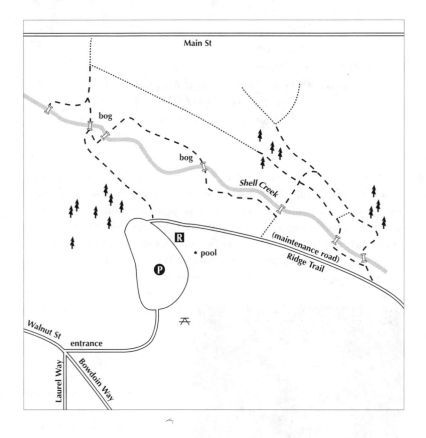

# #15
# TERRACE CREEK PARK

| | |
|---|---|
| HIGHLIGHTS | *Stream, forested ravine* |
| TRAIL | *1.5 miles one way, plus spurs; paved and gravel* |
| OTHER USAGE | *Bicycles* |
| STEEPNESS | *Gentle to steep* |
| CONNECTING TRAILS | *None* |
| PARK SERVICES | *Restrooms, picnic shelter, playground, disc golf course, playing fields* |
| DISABLED ACCESS | *Restrooms and paved trail* |

IN THIS SMALL NEIGHBORHOOD PARK, THE TRAIL GENTLY ASCENDS A peaceful strip of forest in a ravine below suburban Mountlake Terrace. Beginning as a paved walkway by the playground lawn, the trail soon changes to more rugged gravel and climbs moderately into the stately second-growth forest. Terrace Creek murmurs softly alongside. Deep in the wooded ravine, the air is still and quiet. Winter wrens hop from bush to bush and woodpeckers tap old snags for their beetles and bugs.

**Stinging nettle: admire from afar**

Side trails lead to ridgetop homes invisible behind summer growth.

The strange, open, metal "trash containers" throughout the park are in fact holes for disc golf, a game of skill for those adept at tossing Frisbee-like discs long distances. Most of the disc course is along spur trails on the sides of the steep ravine. It's interesting

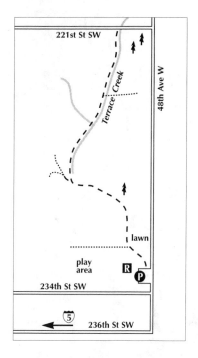

**Nasty Nettle or Yummy Veggie?**

*Nettles make a tasty vegetable, rich in vitamins, if cut young and steamed up for supper. But most of us meet them on the trail—on a tender bit of leg or arm. When brushed, the plant's little hairs break off, injecting formic acid—the same stuff we hate from biting ants. Natural antidotes? Some say rubbing the brown spores of the sword fern on the spot helps. Others say the juice from the stem of wild impatiens (jewelweed) does the trick. If you don't normally have any baking soda with you, try the rubbing. It might work.*

*Native Americans used to flail themselves with stinging nettle to stay awake while out fishing all night on the Sound. Ouch!*

to imagine the contortions necessary to retrieve stray discs from the thickets of blackberry and nettle.

The main trail ends when it reaches 221st Street SW, but additional walking can be had up the side trails and back down.

*How to Get There:* From I-5 south of Everett, northbound, take exit 178 (236th St SW, Mountlake Terrace). Turn right (east) on 236th St SW. Go about 0.8 mile and turn left (north) on 48th Ave W. The park is on your left at the corner of 48th Ave W and 233rd St SW.

From I-5 south of Everett, southbound, take exit 179 (220th St SW, Mountlake Terrace). Turn left (east) onto 220th St SW. Turn right (south) on 56th Ave W then left (east) on 236th St SW and proceed as above. Mountlake Terrace Parks (206) 776-9173.

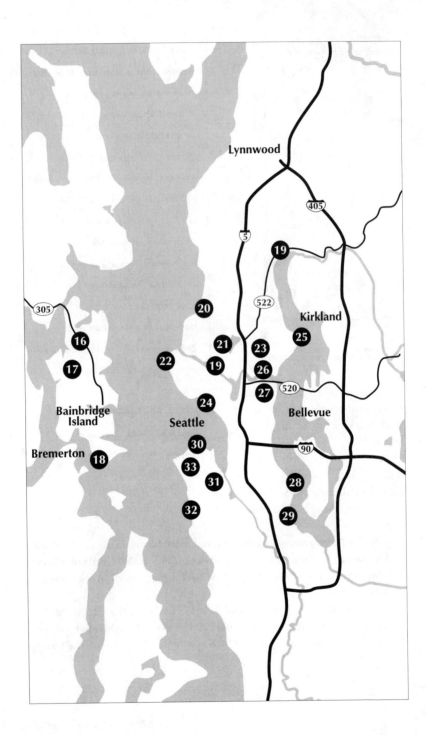

# IN AND AROUND SEATTLE

# #16
# MANZANITA PARK

BAINBRIDGE ISLAND, 13.5 MILES WEST OF SEATTLE (INCLUDING FERRY)

| | |
|---|---|
| HIGHLIGHTS | *Forest, wetlands* |
| TRAIL | *2.3 miles total; natural surface* |
| OTHER USAGE | *Horses (some separate trails); no bicycles* |
| STEEPNESS | *Gentle to steep* |
| CONNECTING TRAILS | *None* |
| PARK SERVICES | *Restrooms, sketch map of trails, brochure, horse jumps* |
| DISABLED ACCESS | *None* |

BROAD, SMOOTH TRAILS LOOP THROUGHOUT THIS QUIET FOREST OF Sitka spruce, western yew, Douglas fir, maple, and alder. But these trails are not for hikers only. In fact, large equestrian cross-country jumps straddle the trail like bizarre roadblocks. If you choose a trail with a narrow gate, you'll enter walkers-only land, with steeper terrain, more intimate forest, and a wetland.

Though the park is owned by the City of Bainbridge Island, many of the upper trails in Manzanita are maintained by the Saddle Club, which owns adjoining land. Most days of the year you'll be safe walking these horse-jumping trails. But always listen for the thundering of hooves as the horses and riders barrel along to clear the solid wood jumps. On events days (weekends only, spring through fall), the parking lot will be crowded and the mobs of people and horses will forewarn you. Better, perhaps, to put off the walk and join the spectators on the sidelines to watch the horses perform.

**Sharing the Trail with Horses:**

*Horses like to know you're there, but they don't like sudden noises or motions. Step to the side, or walk single file. Say "Hi," so they don't think you're an old stump that suddenly moves.*

*34* 🐾 **TAKE A WALK**

The pedestrian trailhead is just before the parking lot, and takes you through a narrow gate—obviously meant to exclude horses. (They have their own entrances.) A multitrunked western red cedar greets you, its branches gracefully curved upward and low enough to rest on. Pastel blue lichen coats the trunk. At a T junction you meet the first of several loops of equestrian trails. Turn right to explore the northern section, where the horses must perform in narrow glens of cedar and Douglas fir trees. Drop down through a gated trail to another walkers-only path.

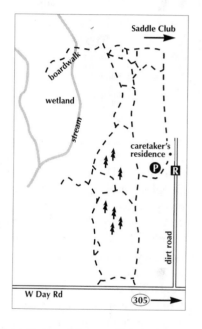

Winding along a hillside, you can look out into the middle story of a ravine filled with bigleaf maples and madronas.

At the bottom of the ravine, an old boardwalk leads into the marsh. Plans are under way to renovate it but, until then, you might find parts of it slippery, broken, or blocked by fallen trees. The wetland trail is not a loop, so explore the skunk-cabbage country, where salamanders slide in slime and Pacific tree frogs sing, and then return to the upper trails of the park.

*How to Get There:* From Seattle take the ferry to Bainbridge Island. Head north out of Winslow on SR 305. Go 4.3 miles and turn left on W Day Rd. In 0.4 mile turn right on a dirt road signposted for the park. Look on the left for a trailhead sign in 0.3 mile, then a parking area.

From Bremerton, take SR 3 north to Poulsbo. Turn south on SR 305 to Bainbridge Island. Turn right on W Day Rd and proceed as above. Bainbridge Island Parks (206) 842-2306.

# #17
# THE GRAND FOREST

**BAINBRIDGE ISLAND, 12.5 MILES WEST OF SEATTLE (INCLUDING FERRY)**

| | |
|---|---|
| HIGHLIGHTS | *Forest, bird-watching* |
| TRAIL | *8.2 miles total (5.4 in Mandus Olson section, 2.8 in Miller Road section); natural surface* |
| OTHER USAGE | *Bicycles, horses* |
| STEEPNESS | *Gentle to steep* |
| CONNECTING TRAILS | *None* |
| PARK SERVICES | *Picnic area* |
| DISABLED ACCESS | *None* |

SOFT DIRT TRAILS QUILT THIS OPEN FOREST OF DOUGLAS FIR IN LARGE, easy loops. Silence is broken by the sudden birdlike chatter of the tawny Douglas squirrels that patrol the tree trunks and branches like overzealous guardians of the woods.

Bainbridge's Grand Forest comprises three separate areas, acquired from the Department of Natural Resources in 1990. Only two currently have developed walking trails. In the Mandus Olson block, map signs along the trail with "You are here" dots help steer you around the loops. If your sense of direction is anything less than that of a migrating bird, you'll be glad they're there. So uniform is this forest that without the guidance of low, slanted sunshine it is easy to get turned around. In the southeastern corner a shallow ravine extends to the east, a deep cradle of fern and shrub. Elsewhere, the understory shrubbery is low enough to give a clear view of the middle layer of polelike trunks, character-

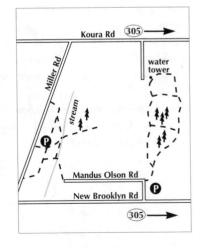

istic of a farmed forest. Above it all spreads the upper story of Douglas fir boughs. With the openness come great bird-watching possibilities: easy viewing to the tops of shrubs, and a chance to see woodpeckers, nuthatches, and brown creepers on the trunks.

In the more recently developed trail system of the Grand Forest section off Miller Road, you can explore a spiderweb of loops in a denser, more varied forest. Bigleaf maple and red alder mix with Douglas fir and western red cedar, and the eastern part is highlighted

Stately Douglas fir trunks in the Grand Forest

by a small stream and surrounding wetland. Two parallel trails lead north and south, with tributary paths joining them. Next to the westernmost one is a picnic table. Huge stumps border the trail, doing their work as nurseries for saplings.

*How to Get There:* **From Seattle take the ferry to Bainbridge Island. Head north out of Winslow on SR 305. To reach the Mandus Olson section, go 1.6 miles north and turn left on Sportsman Club Rd. After the school, turn right on New Brooklyn Rd. Go 1.3 miles and turn right on Mandus Olson Rd. Park where the road makes a sharp left turn. Limited parking.**

**To reach the Miller Rd section with 5 miles of trails, return to New Brooklyn Rd and turn right (west). Go 0.75 mile and turn right on Miller Rd. Just past the Bainbridge Gardens Nursery (on the left) look on the right at the top of a rise for a sign for The Grand Forest. Two pull-outs provide limited parking. Bainbridge Island Parks (206) 842-2306.**

# #18
# FORT WARD STATE PARK

**Bainbridge Island, on Puget Sound, 16 miles west of Seattle
(including ferry)**

| | |
|---|---|
| HIGHLIGHTS | *Saltwater beach, Olympic mountain views, bird-watching, forest, historical site* |
| TRAIL | *About 1.3-mile loop; paved and natural surfaces* |
| OTHER USAGE | *Bicycles (on paved shoreline path only)* |
| STEEPNESS | *Level to steep* |
| CONNECTING TRAILS | *Fort Ward Historical Area, via roads (ask ranger for information)* |
| PARK SERVICES | *Restrooms, picnic tables, interpretive signs, gun battery ruins, viewing blinds, boat launch* |
| DISABLED ACCESS | *Upper parking lot, restrooms, picnic area; paved shore trail (Pleasant Beach Drive)* |

ALTHOUGH IT WAS AN EXTENSIVE MILITARY HOLDING AT THE TURN OF the century, not much remains of the original Fort Ward. Today, the appeal of this state park lies in its sylvan tranquillity and water's-edge walking, rather than its military history. As dense as any second-growth Northwest forest, the ferns and towering bigleaf maples enclose walkers in a green cocoon.

Cormorants perch on pilings offshore

If you park at the boat launch at the northern end of the gated Pleasant Beach Drive, you can warm up with a stroll along the 4,300-foot paved trail bordering

Rich Passage. To one side, sword fern and horsetail vie for space beneath the hulking limbs of bigleaf maples and western red cedars. By the water, delicate white snowberries and wild roses line the path in late summer. Short spur trails lead to blinds for observing the herons, cormorants, loons, and maybe harbor seals on the water.

At the southern end of the road, past the bird blind, you can ascend the steep paved trail to the upper picnic area. From here, if the ground is not too muddy, head down the half-mile natural-surface trail back to the lower parking lot. Along the way you can search the forest trees for Steller's jays and winter wrens. Don't leave the trail though; poison oak, an uncommon plant in the Northwest, lurks in the undergrowth—green in summer, red in fall.

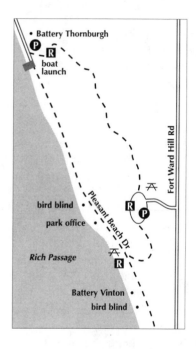

At high or low tide the best walking may be along the almost-mile-long beach, from which you can more easily smell the fresh salt air, watch ferries negotiate the narrow Rich Passage, and observe the antics of the double-crested cormorants as they stretch and preen on the offshore pilings.

***How to Get There:*** From Seattle take the ferry to Bainbridge Island. Head north out of Winslow on SR 305. Go 1 mile and turn left on High School Rd. Follow the brown state park signs. In summer you can choose to enter the upland picnic area (Fort Ward Hill Rd) or the boat launch area (Pleasant Beach Dr). In winter, only the boat launch area is open for parking.

From Bremerton, take Hwy 3 north to Poulsbo. Turn south on SR 305 to Bainbridge Island. Follow the brown state park signs to Fort Ward. Washington State Parks (206) 842-4041.

# #19
# BURKE-GILMAN TRAIL

KENMORE (12 MILES NORTH OF SEATTLE) TO SEATTLE
(BALLARD DISTRICT, 5 MILES NORTH OF DOWNTOWN)

| | |
|---|---|
| HIGHLIGHTS | *Lakeshore, parks, art, views, historical site* |
| TRAIL | *16.5 miles one way; paved* |
| OTHER USAGE | *Bicycles* |
| STEEPNESS | *Level to gentle* |
| CONNECTING TRAILS | *Sammamish River Trail (Walk #34), Magnuson Park (Walk #25), other parks* |
| PARK SERVICES | *Restrooms, picnic shelters, beaches* |
| DISABLED ACCESS | *Restrooms, picnic areas, trail* |

SNAKING ALONG THE SHORE OF LAKE WASHINGTON AND INTO THE Ballard district of Seattle, this 14-mile, paved corridor of off-road walking meets the needs of those who seek the freedom of the trail just blocks from home.

Beginning in Seattle's Ballard district on 8th Avenue NW, the trail follows the original grade of the Seattle, Lake Shore & Eastern Railroad, which, almost a century later, under the ownership of Burlington Northern, was abandoned in 1971. Seven years later, Seattle opened the Burke-Gilman (named in honor of the original railroad's founders) as an off-road, multiuse trail. Near the western end, the trail passes Gas Works Park, a mini-walk in itself, with views of Lake Union and downtown Seattle, then continues east through the University of Washington campus and past Magnuson Park (Walk # 25). Enjoy the fall colors of the hazelnut trees and bigleaf maples along this stretch.

North from here, increasing greenery lines the trail, which often runs between backyards, well landscaped with both native and exotic trees and shrubs. You get peek-a-boo views of Lake Washington, but the best is saved for the far north. Blackberries line the trail, providing spring color and fragrance and summer snacking. Two miles east of Tracy Owen Station in Kenmore, the trail changes to the Sammamish River Trail (Walk # 34). Here you can enjoy a beach, a green lawn, and views south across Lake Washington.

One warning: the trail is heavily used by bicyclists and in-line skaters. Always walk on the right—in single file if it's a busy weekend. Toddlers and impatient children might do better on a quieter trail.

*How to Get There:* The best access points with parking are: Magnuson Park (Walk #25), Gas Works Park, or Tracy Owen Station (Log Boom Park).

To reach Gas Works Park: From I-5 in Seattle, north- or southbound, take exit 169 (NE 45th St). Go west on NE 45th St and turn left (south) on Stone Way. Follow Stone Way to Lake Union and turn left on N Northlake Way. Parking is on the right.

To reach Tracy Owen Station: From I-5 in Seattle, northbound, take exit 171 (SR 522, Bothell, Lake City Way). Go north 6.5 miles and turn right in Kenmore on 61st Ave NE into the park.

From I-405 north of Bellevue, northbound, take exit 23 (SR 522 west, Bothell, Seattle). Southbound take exit 23B (SR 522 west, Bothell). Go west on SR 522 about 4.4 miles and turn left on 61st Ave NE into the park. Trail brochure shows other access points. Seattle Parks (206) 684-4075.

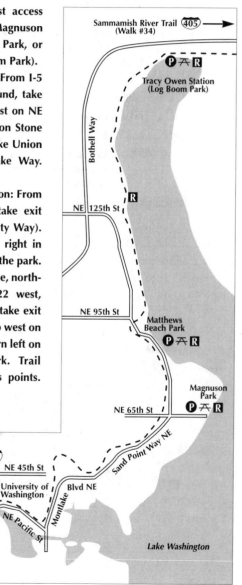

# #20
# CARKEEK PARK

**SEATTLE, ON PUGET SOUND, 8 MILES NORTH OF DOWNTOWN**

| | |
|---|---|
| HIGHLIGHTS | *Saltwater beach, forested ravine, Olympic views, salmon-spawning creek* |
| TRAIL | *1-mile ravine walk, one way; several miles of side trails; natural surface* |
| OTHER USAGE | *Bicycles* |
| STEEPNESS | *Gentle to moderate* |
| CONNECTING TRAILS | *None* |
| PARK SERVICES | *Restrooms, picnic shelters, Environmental Education Center, playgrounds, model airplane field* |
| DISABLED ACCESS | *Restrooms* |

LEAVE COMMERCIAL SEATTLE BEHIND AS YOU WIND DOWN EITHER ROAD or footpath into this verdant ravine where moss clings to the bigleaf maples and old logs straddle Piper's Creek. Like other ravines along the

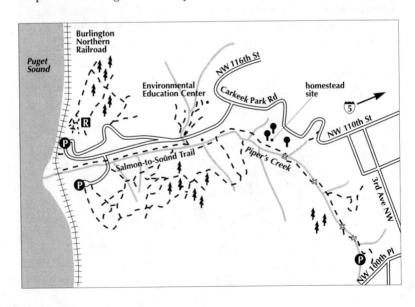

Sound, this one enchants with the steady downward flow of several small streams, the surprising gurgles of miniature waterfalls, and the profuse undergrowth of the forest.

In spring the trailside is lush with salmonberry bushes, the fruit still yellow and orange, awaiting the summer sun. Incredibly large stumps, too big to hug, provide nutrients for young salal bushes and Douglas firs. But all is not wild here. The old orchard remains as testimony to the early settlers A. W. Piper and his wife, Minna, who supplied produce to downtown Seattle from this homestead in the late 1800s.

In the lower parking area, look for the footbridge leading over the train tracks to the watery world of Puget Sound. The call of the whinnying robins is replaced by the call of gulls, and your eyes are no longer drawn to branches overhead but further away to the lofty Olympics in the west, or to your feet where the beach sand ripples under the retreating tide.

> **Trees Wanted—Dead or Alive:**
>
> *When you see a downed log or an old snag or stump, think of all the years it lived before it fell or burned. And look at all the life it supports now that it's dead.*

*How to Get There:* From I-5 in Seattle, north- or southbound, take exit 173 (Northgate Way, 1st Ave NE). If northbound, turn left on 1st Ave NE, then left on N Northgate Way and go under the freeway. If southbound, go right on N Northgate Way (which becomes NE 105th St). Go 8 or 9 blocks and turn right on Greenwood Ave N. Go 2 blocks and turn left on NW 110th St (which becomes Carkeek Park Rd and winds down to the lower parking lot). Gates close at 9 PM.

To access the trail at the top of the park, stay on NE 105th St as it veers left to become Holman Rd NW. Go 2 blocks and turn right on 3rd Ave NW. Go 1 block and turn left on NW 100th Pl to the small picnic/parking area. Seattle Parks (206) 684-0877.

# #21
# GREEN LAKE

SEATTLE, **4.5** MILES NORTH OF DOWNTOWN

| | |
|---|---|
| HIGHLIGHTS | *Lake, bird-watching* |
| TRAIL | *2.8-mile loop; paved* |
| OTHER USAGE | *Bicycles (in a designated lane)* |
| STEEPNESS | *Level* |
| CONNECTING TRAILS | *Woodland Park trails (across street)* |
| PARK SERVICES | *Restrooms, wading pool, beach, concessions, community center, playing fields, theater, boating (non-motorized), fishing piers* |
| DISABLED ACCESS | *Restrooms, buildings, trail* |

CIRCLE THIS PEACEFUL LAKE ON A DEFINED 2.8-MILE PAVED TRAIL AND meet a cross-section of Seattle life. Year-round, Green Lake attracts families, dog-walkers, joggers, bicyclists, the old and the young—all out to enjoy this strip of greenery in the 260-acre park. In spring, walk beneath flowering cherry and dogwood trees. In fall, look for the red berries on the hawthorns.

No matter the time of year, there is activity on the lake: summer paddleboaters, small sailboats, wind surfers or the action of winter wind on water kicking up the whitecaps. Two nature-preserve islands provide shelter for many birds, but are inaccessible to walkers except through the magic of binoculars. Fall, winter, and spring are the best times to see the migratory birds such as buffleheads and white-fronted geese. Year-round, the omnipresent mallards and Canada geese forage in the reeds by the lake's edge, and red-winged blackbirds add a splash of color to the scene.

**Walkers and joggers hit the trail**

Because of its popularity, traffic flow is regulated on the paved trail: walkers (including those with baby strollers) take the inside half and can travel either direction, while those on wheels must stick to a counter-clockwise direction on the outer half.

*How to Get There:* From I-5 in Seattle, north- or southbound, take exit 169 (NE 50th St) and head west (left if northbound, right if southbound). Go about 0.8 mile to Green Lake Way N, turn right and park along the street by the lake, or in lots farther north. Alternatively, continue on NE 50th St to park near the tennis courts. (This also allows easy access to the wooded trails and hillsides of Woodland Park.) Seattle Parks (206) 684-4075.

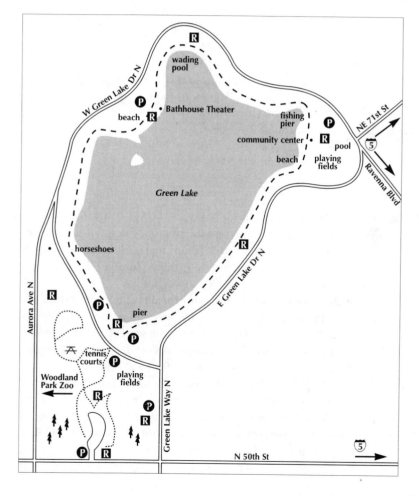

# #22
# DISCOVERY PARK

SEATTLE, ON PUGET SOUND, 6 MILES NORTHWEST OF DOWNTOWN

| | |
|---|---|
| HIGHLIGHTS | *Saltwater beach, forest, meadow, wetlands, historical site, bird-watching, views, art* |
| TRAIL | *7 miles (including 1/2-mile Nature Trail and 2.8-mile Loop Trail) plus 2 miles of beach; paved, gravel, and natural surfaces* |
| OTHER USAGE | *Pedestrians only on Loop Trail and Wolf Tree Nature Trail (no dogs on Wolf Tree); bicycles on paved roadways only* |
| STEEPNESS | *Gentle to steep* |
| CONNECTING TRAILS | *None* |
| PARK SERVICES | *Restrooms, interpretive center, playgrounds, picnic tables, courts, maps, brochures, classes; Daybreak Star Arts Center (206) 285-4425* |
| DISABLED ACCESS | *Restrooms, buildings; Pass available to drive to beach* |

WALK A WIND-SWEPT BLUFF BY A GRASSY MEADOW, HUNT GHOST SHRIMP on the beach, or search the treetops for an eagle's nest. With 7 miles of trails to tread, Seattle's largest park (more than 500 acres), presents a variety of urban wilderness habitats to explore from beach to meadow to wetland to forest.

Start at the Visitor Center (east gate) for maps, then set off on the Loop Trail to the west. Crossing the flower-strewn meadow, watch for violet-green swallows in summer, or listen for the screech of hawks in winter. The old buildings are what remain of Fort Lawton, and they're worth exploring when you're in the mood for local history.

From the sandy bluff, listen for foghorns and the barks of sea lions, and watch the vessels ply the Sound far below. If the wind is from the south, head down the forested trail to South Beach. (The goal being to stay upwind of the Metro sewage treatment plant on the headland.) The trail is steep, with steps and observation platforms. On the log-lined tidal flats children love poking about the mucky sand for crabs and

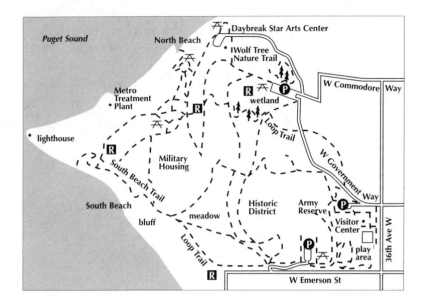

clams and squiggly creatures. Geology buffs can study the 300-foot cliffs for clues to our glaciated past.

Back on the Loop Trail, stick to the larger, marked trails. Later, as you become familiar with the layout, you can explore the shortcuts and side trails with confidence. At the north parking lot, leave time for the half-mile nature trail, which features interpretive signs and peaceful walking.

*How to Get There:* From I-5 in Seattle, northbound, take the left lane exit 167 (Mercer St, Seattle Center) and follow signs for the Seattle Center. At the Pacific Science Center turn right on Denny Way, which veers right to become Elliott Ave at the waterfront. From here go 1.2 miles to the Garfield St Bridge where Elliott Ave becomes 15th Ave W. Continue north on 15th Ave W 1 mile and exit right for Dravus St and turn left (west). Immediately after crossing the railroad yards turn right on 20th Ave W which merges into Gilman Ave W. Bear left onto W Fort St which becomes W Government Way and will lead into the park.

From I-5 north of downtown Seattle, southbound, take exit 169 (NE 50th St). Turn right on NE 50th St and go about 1.7 miles (past the zoo) until it merges (to the right) onto NW Market St. Turn left on 15th Ave NW, cross the Ballard Bridge and take the first exit on the right (Fisherman's Terminal/Emerson). Emerson merges to the right onto Gilman Ave W. Proceed as above.

Organized groups and cars with children under 5 or people over 62 can drive to the beach. Seattle Parks (206) 386-4236.

# #23
# RAVENNA PARK

**SEATTLE, 6.5 MILES NORTHEAST OF DOWNTOWN**

| | |
|---|---|
| HIGHLIGHTS | *Forested ravine, stream* |
| TRAIL | *1.5 miles total; natural surface* |
| OTHER USAGE | *Bicycles on 5-foot-wide paths only* |
| STEEPNESS | *Level to steep* |
| CONNECTING TRAILS | *None* |
| PARK SERVICES | *Restrooms, picnic tables, tennis courts, wading pool* |
| DISABLED ACCESS | *None* |

THIS SECRET CLEFT OF CHOICE GREENERY IN THE MIDST OF URBAN
Seattle offers some of the quietest, most treasured walking in the city. In
fair weather, the steep side trails, the paths along the rims, and the wide
trail in the ravine are filled with hikers, joggers, and dog-walkers. Even
in winter, when a dusting of snow coats the trail, footprints still tell of

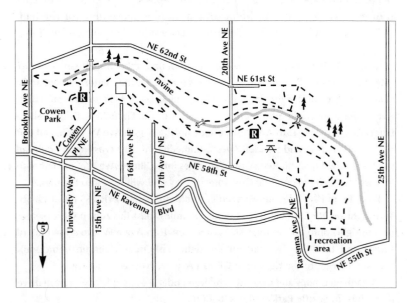

dedicated Ravenna-lovers out to enjoy their park despite slippery trails and a partially frozen stream.

One of Seattle's oldest parks—acquired before the 1909 Alaska-Yukon-Pacific Exposition—Ravenna has seen bad years and good. Known at midcentury as a squatter's haven, it was later cleaned up and has now become a magnet park for Seattleites.

From the massive footbridge (20th Avenue NE) over the ravine and the rim trails where wild roses and berry bushes bloom, you look out into the canopy of immense red alder and maple. As you descend the angled trails that traverse the hillside, the vegetation changes to a mix of native and ornamental trees (yew, redwood, Pacific dogwood, Douglas fir), sheltering an undergrowth of fern and salal. Leaning madrona trees form intricate patterns with their peeling bark branches.

Once in the ravine, you have no sense of city, no sight of houses. The stream flows from west to east, heading for Lake Washington. Working its way around boulders and logs, it brings nutrients to the skunk cabbages and stream creatures that live in its water and along its banks.

This Isn't New York! *Try saying "Hi." You may not talk to strangers on the street, but a camaraderie develops among walkers. Some neighborhood trails have been responsible for creating whole new social groups.*

*How to Get There:* From I-5 in Seattle, take exit 169 (NE 50th St) and head east (right if northbound, left if southbound). Turn left onto 11th Ave NE, then, in 4 blocks, turn right onto Ravenna Blvd. Park on the street near Cowen Park and walk up Cowen Pl NE to Ravenna Park.

Alternatively, northbound on I-5 only, take exit 170 (Ravenna Blvd, NE 65th St) and go right on Ravenna Blvd to Cowen Park (or stay on Ravenna Blvd to the recreational end of Ravenna Park). Seattle Parks (206) 684-4075.

# #24
# MYRTLE EDWARDS AND ELLIOTT BAY PARKS

SEATTLE, ON PUGET SOUND, 2 MILES NORTH OF DOWNTOWN

| | |
|---|---|
| HIGHLIGHTS | *Olympic views, beach, art* |
| TRAIL | *1.25 miles one way; paved* |
| OTHER USAGE | *Bicycles (on a separate path)* |
| STEEPNESS | *Level* |
| CONNECTING TRAILS | *Elliott Bay Bikeway (via north end of Elliott Bay Park)* |
| PARK SERVICES | *Restrooms, fishing pier, concessions* |
| DISABLED ACCESS | *Restrooms, fishing pier, concessions, trail* |

THIS NECKLACE OF GREEN SO CLOSE TO DOWNTOWN SEATTLE offers fresh salt air, an ever-changing view of vessels on the Sound, and peaceful walking since wheels and feet are segregated on separate trails. Landscaped with roses, lawns, and low shrubs, this strip of garden park attracts walkers for sunrise glow on the Olympics, fresh air at midday, and sunset views of the last golden light on Mount Rainier. After dark, the lighted pier attracts fishing and crabbing aficionados.

Offshore you may see sea lions, harbor seals, and numerous waterfowl, especially in the fall and winter. Occasionally, too, a river otter pads along a tiny beach, clambers over rocks, then slithers back to do rolls and otter-wheelies in the cold salt water of the Sound.

Here nature and industry blend in a fine harmony: The setting sun puts the gigantic grain terminal in silhouette against the Olympics. The cacophony of seagulls resounds above the drone of a foghorn and Mount Rainier asserts its majesty over the city's skyline.

Stroll the whole length of the two parks, or a bit from either end. The grass is interrupted by a carefully laid out gravel canvas upon which artist Michael Heizer created his immense rock and concrete sculpture, *Adjacent, Against, Upon.* Just north of the boundary between Myrtle Edwards and Elliott Bay Parks, Shipmate's Light stands in honor and memory of those lost at sea.

*How to Get There:* From I-5 in Seattle, north- or southbound, take exit 167 (Mercer St/Seattle Center). Follow signs for the Seattle Center, staying on Broad St past the Center, which will take you to the waterfront. Turn right onto Alaskan Way and drive to its end. Park here, near Pier 70, for Myrtle Edwards.

For free parking at Elliott Bay Park, turn right on Elliott Ave from Broad St. Go about 1.5 miles and turn left on W Galer St. Cross the railroad tracks and proceed straight to the water. (Alternatively, after crossing the tracks follow Trail signs to the left, which will put you near the fishing pier.) Open dawn to 10 or 11 PM for night fishing. Myrtle Edwards is administered by Seattle Parks (206) 684-4075. Elliott Bay is administered by Port of Seattle (206) 728-3000.

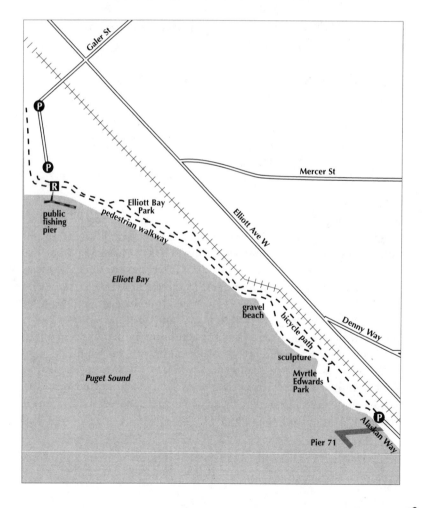

# #25
# MAGNUSON PARK AND NOAA WATERFRONT

### SEATTLE, ON LAKE WASHINGTON, 8 MILES NORTHEAST OF DOWNTOWN

| | |
|---|---|
| HIGHLIGHTS | *Lakeshore, meadows, art, Cascade views, off-leash area, beach* |
| TRAIL | *About 3 miles total; paved, gravel, and natural surfaces* |
| OTHER USAGE | *Bicycles (except on NOAA trail, which is pedestrians only)* |
| STEEPNESS | *Level* |
| CONNECTING TRAILS | *Burke-Gilman Trail (Walk #19), via streets* |
| PARK SERVICES | *Restrooms, picnic areas, playing fields, tennis courts, boat launch* |
| DISABLED ACCESS | *Restrooms, picnic areas, shoreline trail in Magnuson Park* |

STILL CALLED SAND POINT FROM ITS FORMER DAYS AS A NAVAL STATION, Magnuson Park is one of the brightest parks in the Seattle area, with 200 acres of open meadows and lakeshore walking. Purchased from the Navy in 1975, the park has seen years of improvement since the bleak days when it smelled of aviation fuel. To increase the greenery, the city originally planted trees, many of which died from lack of water. Now the park's pastoral setting is part of its allure, and any future plantings call for native shrubs, not trees. Only the southern end has a forested hillside with dirt trails; elsewhere, be prepared for sun and wind.

Blustery days offer entertainment as you walk the wide aggregate trail from south to north. Windsurfers race from the headland onto the wind-whipped lake, and kite-flying aficionados battle their colorful winged creatures from the hillock.

If you come with a dog, or want to walk in seclusion, follow signs to the western border of the park, where the designated off-leash area (a pilot project through May 1997) is rimmed by luscious summer blackberry thickets. This trail meanders past the playing fields and rejoins the paved, aggregate walkway at the NOAA gate.

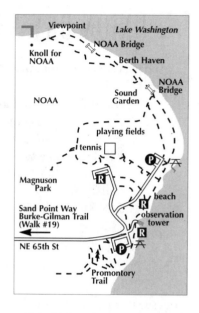

At the end of the pavement a fence with gate marks the boundary of the grounds of the National Oceanic and Atmospheric Administration (NOAA), which are open to the public. Five art-in-the-parks projects here enhance the waterside graveled walk. Stroll across two bridges inscribed with quotes from *Moby Dick*, enjoy views over the lake at *Berth Haven* and *Viewpoint*, guess the artist's intentions for the conical *Knoll for NOAA*, and walk through a haunting, moaning, otherworldly symphony of wind in the *Sound Garden*.

**How to Get There:** From I-5 north of downtown Seattle, north- or southbound, take exit 169 (NE 45th St). Turn east (right if northbound, left if southbound) on NE 45th St and go past the University of Washington, down the viaduct and another 0.5 mile. Bear left onto Sand Point Way N. Turn right on NE 65th St into Magnuson Park. The southern parking lot is straight ahead. Other lots, near the playing fields and beaches, are to the left. The NOAA Waterfront walk extends north from Magnuson Park. Seattle Parks (206) 684-4075. NOAA (206) 526-4548.

# #26
# UNION BAY NATURAL AREAS

SEATTLE, ON LAKE WASHINGTON, 5 MILES NORTHEAST OF DOWNTOWN

| | |
|---|---|
| HIGHLIGHTS | *Meadows, wetlands, ponds, bird-watching* |
| TRAIL | *1.5 miles total with loops north and south; gravel and natural surfaces* |
| OTHER USAGE | *Bicycles on Wahkiakum Lane; pedestrians only elsewhere* |
| STEEPNESS | *Level* |
| CONNECTING TRAILS | *None* |
| PARK SERVICES | *None* |
| DISABLED ACCESS | *None* |

THIS SWATH OF UNTAMED GREENERY BETWEEN HUSKY STADIUM AND THE Center for Urban Horticulture is a stopover for thousands of migrating waterfowl and other birds on the Pacific Flyway. Come in fall, winter, or spring, when the ponds may host ruddy ducks, hooded mergansers, and green- or blue-winged teals. The trees and bushes may be dotted with goldfinches, vireos, and waxwings. In summer the meadows are bright with yellow Scotch broom and blue chicory. All year long, mute swans glide on the calm waters of Union Bay, while Swainson's hawks hunt overhead, and muskrats make their homes in Shoveler's Pond.

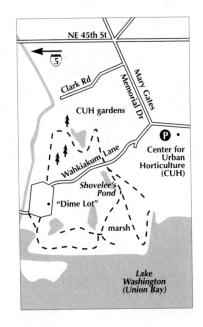

Before 1916 this was another cove of Lake Washington, but when the Ship Canal was built the water receded and the land slowly adapted to its dry status. It's now an ecological research area, and walkers are welcome provided they keep pets on leash and walk only on established paths. From Wahkiakum Lane, take the first left onto a wood-chip trail, which passes the seasonal Shoveler's Pond (dry in summer) and then crosses the meadow to the lakeshore. Stay alert for ring-tailed pheasants in the grass and the shadow of eagles overhead. Several small paths weave through the cattails at the water's edge. In summer these are practically impassable due to blackberry invasion, but in winter you can find tiny clearings from which you can watch the lake-loving waterfowl.

Continue on the paths around the other ponds, where you may see plovers and bitterns. New plantings of dogwood and other trees enhance the seclusion and help ensure the repeated return of the seasonal migrants. This is a walk for nature observers and for those who find pleasure in the wildlife surprises that each day brings.

*How to Get There:* From I-5 north of downtown Seattle , north- or southbound, take exit 169 (NE 45th St). Turn east (right if northbound, left if southbound) on NE 45th St and go past the University of Washington and down the viaduct, staying on NE 45th St. Take the first right after University Village on Mary Gates Memorial Way where signs point to the Center for Urban Horticulture (CUH). Park along the road and walk from the west end of the CUH parking lot onto Wahkiakum Lane into the preserve.

From the Eastside, cross Lake Washington on the SR 520 Bridge. Take the Montlake exit (north) and turn right on Montlake Blvd. Stay to the right, passing the Husky Stadium and merging with NE 45th St. Turn right on Mary Gates Memorial Way and proceed as above. University of Washington, Center for Urban Horticulture (206)543-8616.

# 27

# WASHINGTON PARK ARBORETUM

**SEATTLE, ON LAKE WASHINGTON, 4 MILES EAST OF DOWNTOWN**

| | |
|---|---|
| HIGHLIGHTS | *Arboretum, gardens, wetlands, bird-watching* |
| TRAIL | *Waterfront 0.5 mile one way; garden paths at least 4 miles; natural surface* |
| OTHER USAGE | *Bicycles on paved roads only* |
| STEEPNESS | *Level to gentle* |
| CONNECTING TRAILS | *None* |
| PARK SERVICES | *Restrooms, gift shop, classes, flower shows, playground, interpretive trail, Japanese Garden (admission fee), tennis courts, map, brochures, Visitor Center* |
| DISABLED ACCESS | *Restrooms and Visitor Center; Azalea Way (only when dry)* |

WITH EACH SEASON, COLOR LURES YOU DEEPER INTO THE GRACEFUL elegance of the Arboretum. Spring and summer bring an explosion of red, purple, and yellow rhododendrons, pink and white camellias, and an artist's palette of other perennials; fall's warm tones of orange and yellow brighten the trails. Even in winter, the myriad colors of bark, foliage, and winter berries contrast cheerfully with the drab days; as you walk, look for the striped-bark maples, the tiger bark of the cherries, and the sinewy shapes of trees and shrubs.

First-time visitors may want to get a free map of this 200-acre park from the Visitor Center and then set off on Azalea Way, taking small side trips into specialized gardens such as the Winter Garden, the Rhododendron Glen, and the Woodland

**Variegated holly at the Arboretum**

Trail. Meander paths on hillsides planted with exotic trees and shrubs. Cross the old stone bridge to the Pinetum for the pungent scent of fir and pine.

Along the Waterfront Trail bordering Lake Washington, wildlife abounds. Here you'll find mallards, coots, and grebes. In spring the tree swallows swoop and dive for insects above the marsh and in the evenings return to their nesting boxes along the trail. Canada geese nest on the hummocks beneath the reeds and cattails. Test your knowledge of marsh plants with the self-guiding tour booklet that illustrates many of the common plants seen here. Whatever your reason for walking, this mature and well-loved park, dating back to 1934, provides constantly changing botanical treasures on its interlacing trails.

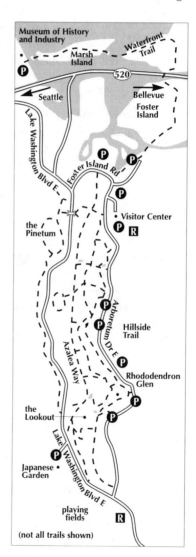

***How to Get There:*** From I-5 in Seattle, north-or southbound, take exit 168B (SR 520, Bellevue). Take the first exit (Montlake) from SR 520. Cross Montlake Blvd and wind down the hill to the T junction at Lake Washington Blvd E. Turn left and then right into the Arboretum. Visitor Center is on your left.

From the Eastside, take the SR 520 Bridge over Lake Washington. Take the first Seattle exit (Lake Washington Blvd). At the end of the ramp turn left, then left again at the T junction at Lake Washington Blvd E. Take the next right into the Arboretum. Visitor Center is on your left. Free park maps available. Arboretum Visitor Center information (206) 543-8800.

# #28
# SEWARD PARK

SEATTLE, ON LAKE WASHINGTON, 6 MILES SOUTHEAST OF DOWNTOWN

| | |
|---|---|
| HIGHLIGHTS | *Lakeshore, old-growth forest, views, bird-watching, beach* |
| TRAIL | *2.5-mile shore loop, paved; 1 mile one way, natural surface* |
| OTHER USAGE | *Bicycles on paved trail; pedestrians only on natural forest trail* |
| STEEPNESS | *Level to gentle* |
| CONNECTING TRAILS | *None* |
| PARK SERVICES | *Restrooms, picnic shelters, fishing pier, amphitheater, art studio* |
| DISABLED ACCESS | *Restrooms, picnic shelter, paved trail* |

SEATTLE'S LARGEST TRACT OF OLD-GROWTH FOREST CROWNS THIS THUMB-shaped peninsula jutting into Lake Washington. Acquired by the city in 1911 as an island, Seward Park was transformed into a peninsula when the lake receded as a result of the building of the Ship Canal in 1916.

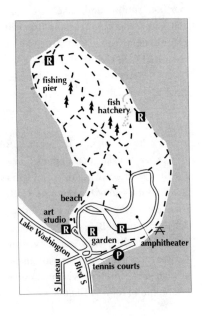

Deep in this forest of immense, pre-Colonial western red cedar, western hemlock, and Douglas fir, varied thrushes call in winter, and in spring the forest comes alive with mating songs and calls of the migrant warblers and kinglets. No city sounds impinge on this woodland with its varied undergrowth of sword fern, Oregon grape, thimbleberry, salal, and twinberry. The main trail follows the spine of the gentle ridge, with numerous

The shoreline trail welcomes both feet and wheels

side trails leading out of the forest to the lakeshore loop walk.

The forest trail and the shore are so different that it's hard to believe they're part of the same park. From the quiet tranquillity of the old forest, you emerge to a faster-moving world. On the paved 2.5-mile shore loop, bicycles zoom by and the in-line skaters skate-dance to music in their headphones. But with grassy stretches on either side of the trail, there is plenty of room for everyone.

In fall, the southern part of the shore trail is lined in orange and red feathery sumac, salal, and hedges of snowberries, and the maples flash warm orange and yellow colors against the blue of the lake. Poison oak lurks among the shrubbery; look for its distinctive leaves in sets of three, shiny green in summer and turning red in fall. Tall madrona trees with their beautiful peeling bark accent the trail edges. Standing on the lakeshore in winter you may see a variety of wintering waterfowl such as mergansers, grebes, and wigeons.

*How to Get There:* From I-5 south of downtown Seattle, northbound, take exit 163 (W Seattle Fwy, Columbian Way). Stay right to get on Columbian Way. Go 1.4 miles and turn right on Beacon Ave S. Go about 0.5 mile and turn left on S Orcas St. At the T junction at Lake Washington Blvd S turn right, then immediately left into the park.

From I-5 south of downtown Seattle, southbound, take exit 163A (Columbian Way). Stay left to cross the freeway onto Columbian Way. Proceed as above. Seattle Parks (206) 684-4075.

# #29
# KUBOTA GARDEN

SEATTLE, 7 MILES SOUTHEAST OF DOWNTOWN

| | |
|---|---|
| HIGHLIGHTS | *Japanese garden, native and ornamental plants, ponds, stream, art* |
| TRAIL | *1.5 miles; gravel and natural surfaces* |
| OTHER USAGE | *Pedestrians only* |
| STEEPNESS | *Level to gentle* |
| CONNECTING TRAILS | *None* |
| PARK SERVICES | *Restrooms, picnic tables, map, free guided tours on weekends except in winter* |
| DISABLED ACCESS | *None* |

THIS PUBLIC GARDEN OF EXOTIC PLANTS, WALKWAYS WIDE AND NARROW, waterfalls, and ponds is a place for meditation and quiet strolls. Pleasure comes not only from the visual, but from the almost tactile sense of shape and design.

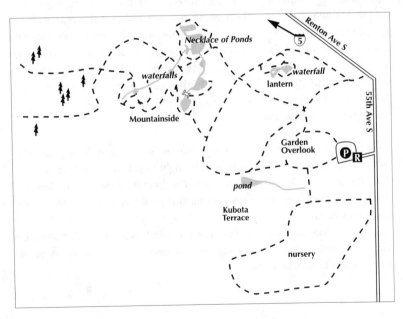

Originally a nursery of 20 acres surrounding an ambitious system of streams and waterfalls, and later donated to Seattle by the Kubota family, the garden continues to provide a place of beauty through form and color, texture and fragrance. Labeling plants was not a priority of the Kubotas, nor is it now. Mature rhododendrons—some 15 feet high and of unknown lineage—bloom in spring, livening the garden with robust color. Migrating songbirds find refuge here, filling the air with their calls. Japanese red and black pines and both yellow and black bamboo grace the paths.

The Moon Bridge arches gracefully over the Necklace of Ponds

This is a garden for meandering, for viewing from all directions. You may have passed the arched Moon Bridge before, but now you tilt your head another way, the sun has dropped lower, and the garden reveals yet another aspect of color, texture, or shape.

Climb the "Mountainside" to enjoy territorial views and perhaps to watch the golden carp in the Necklace of Ponds, 65 feet below.

*How to Get There:* From I-5 south of downtown Seattle, northbound, take exit 157 (M. L. King Way). Follow Martin Luther King Way to S Ryan Way and turn right. At the T junction turn left on 51st Ave S. Turn right on Renton Ave S then right on 55th Ave S. The parking entrance is on the right.

From I-5 south of downtown Seattle, southbound, take exit 161 (Albro Pl, Swift Ave). Turn left on Albro Pl, cross the freeway, and turn right on Swift Ave S. Go 1 mile and turn right on Beacon Ave S. Go 1 mile and turn left on Cloverdale. In 0.5 mile turn right on Renton Ave S then right on 55th Ave S. Kubota Garden Foundation (206) 725-5060. Seattle Parks (206) 684-4584.

# #30
# ALKI BEACH TRAIL

**WEST SEATTLE, ON PUGET SOUND, 5 MILES SOUTHWEST OF DOWNTOWN**

| | |
|---|---|
| HIGHLIGHTS | *Saltwater beach, Olympic and Seattle views* |
| TRAIL | *2.5 miles, paved* |
| OTHER USAGE | *Bicycles; no dogs on beach* |
| STEEPNESS | *Level* |
| CONNECTING TRAILS | *None* |
| PARK SERVICES | *Restrooms, picnic tables, art studio, boat launch* |
| DISABLED ACCESS | *Restrooms, picnic areas, trail* |

LIKE A PROMENADE IN A SOUTH AMERICAN CITY, ALKI BEACH TRAIL stays alive from early morning through the work day and into the evening. Here families, couples, groups, and lone walkers, young and old, stroll the wide, paved trail, dropping into small restaurants and stores and then continuing the promenade along the salt–scented walkway.

Until you know the trail, you may want to drive its length along Harbor Avenue and Alki Avenue SW to the Alki Point Lighthouse. At the western end, the high tide slaps against the retaining wall, creating a chaotic jumble of waves. Wide grassy stretches separate the walking path from the road, making this a safe play and running area for children (but beware the drop to the water off the wall). Picnic tables dot the lawn, and rare hybrid black poplar trees give shade in summer.

**Be a VIP:** *Many city and county parks departments have opportunities for volunteers. In King County, for example, they need people to help with administrative work, data entry, docent programs, fund-raisers, trail restoration, and more. Call your local park authority and ask if they have a VIP (Volunteers In Parks) program. Then get out and help the parks you love.*

It was here, in November 1851, that the Denny Party came ashore to start Seattle's first settlement, which they christened New York Alki, meaning "New York By and By." A monument to their arrival marks the spot.

East from the Alki Bathhouse Art Studio (run by the Alki Community Center), the waterside trail yields to beach. Drift logs, many half buried under sand, make natural benches. At low tide you can explore the mucky tidal flats for shells and pebbles and you may be lucky and see harbor seals lazing about the surface.

East of 55th Avenue the trail more closely borders the road and is raised above the water on a higher wall. From Duwamish Head (the northern tip), watch the night lights of Seattle's skyline create glowing geometrical patterns on the dark sky.

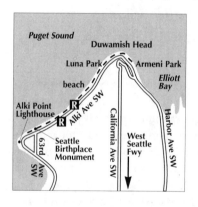

*How to Get There:* From I-5 south of downtown Seattle, northbound, take exit 163 (W Seattle Fwy, Columbian Way) staying left to get on the West Seattle Freeway. Exit onto Harbor Ave SW and follow it north along the water.

From I-5 south of downtown Seattle, southbound, take exit 163A (W Seattle Fwy, Columbian Way) onto the West Seattle Freeway and proceed as above.

The trail begins at Don Armeni Park and Boat Launch, rounds Duwamish Head, then turns west and south to just before the Alki Point at 64th Ave SW. Parking is on the street. Open until 11:30 PM. Seattle Parks (206) 684-4075.

# #31
# CAMP LONG

WEST SEATTLE, 5 MILES SOUTHWEST OF DOWNTOWN

| | |
|---|---|
| HIGHLIGHTS | *Forest, ponds* |
| TRAIL | *2 miles; paved and natural surfaces* |
| OTHER USAGE | *Pedestrians only* |
| STEEPNESS | *Gentle to moderate* |
| CONNECTING TRAILS | *None* |
| PARK SERVICES | *Restrooms, picnic shelters, classes, rock climbing, rustic cabins to rent, camping, maps, brochure, interpretive trail* |
| DISABLED ACCESS | *Restrooms, Rolling Hill Trail, cabins, rock climbing wall* |

WALKING IN CAMP LONG IS LIKE FINDING WILDLANDS IN WEST SEATTLE. The air is fragrant with earth and greenery and sweet forest smells. Although this city park offers overnight camping (the only public camping in Seattle), these 68 acres hold more than cabins and a lodge. They are, for the day hiker, a place of tranquillity and adventure. Beginning at the rustic 1940s lodge, walk left past the cabins to the beginning of the Animal Tracks Nature Trail. This half-mile loop leads past ancient cedar stumps to a newer forest of alder and willow. Plaster casts of raccoon, heron, skunk, coyote, red fox, and squirrel tracks are displayed at the trailhead.

The longer Midwood Loop trail veers off from the nature walk, leading downhill through second-growth forest to the boundary near the golf course. This is a wet trail in winter, but board walkways provide some relief from the mud. Due east of the lodge you come to Polliwog Pond, where turtles bask, salamanders slither, and water insects hatch. If you're lucky you may see hawks, owls, or great blue herons.

The park offers classes on wetlands ecology, forest and pond ecology, and forest dwellers. Special park features include a climbing rock (on which instruction is given by prearrangement) and the "glacier," a concrete/stone structure with handholds and toeholds for climbing and rappelling.

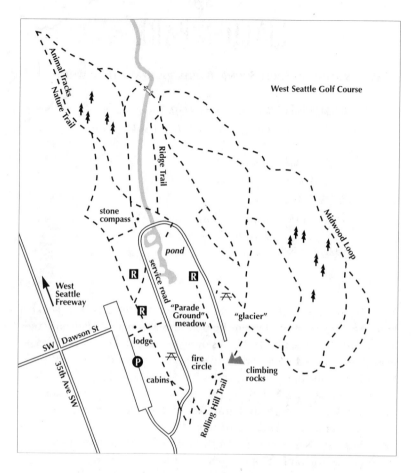

West Seattle Golf Course

Animal Tracks Nature Trail

Ridge Trail

Midwood Loop

stone compass

pond

service road

West Seattle Freeway

R

R

R

"Parade Ground" meadow

"glacier"

SW Dawson St

35th Ave SW

lodge

P

cabins

fire circle

Rolling Hill Trail

climbing rocks

*How to Get There:* From I-5 south of downtown Seattle, northbound, take exit 163 (W Seattle Fwy, Columbian Way) staying left to get on the West Seattle Freeway. Follow it to the end. At the first light off the freeway, turn left onto 35th Ave SW. Go 1 mile and turn left on Dawson St to enter the park.

From I-5 south of downtown Seattle, southbound, take exit 163A (W Seattle Fwy, Columbian Way) onto the West Seattle Freeway and proceed as above. Closed Mondays and Holidays all year, and Sundays in January. Park and trail brochures available. Seattle Parks (206) 684-7434.

# #32
# LINCOLN PARK

| | |
|---|---|
| HIGHLIGHTS | *Saltwater beach, bluff, Olympic views* |
| TRAIL | *4 miles total, including 1 mile on beach; paved and gravel* |
| OTHER USAGE | *Bicycles* |
| STEEPNESS | *Level to steep* |
| CONNECTING TRAILS | *None* |
| PARK SERVICES | *Restrooms, picnic shelters, playgrounds, sports fields, wading pool, swimming pool* |
| DISABLED ACCESS | *Restrooms, picnic areas, paved beach walk* |

FROM HIGH ON THE BLUFF AT LINCOLN PARK THE BARGES AND FERRIES look like large bathtub toys on the smooth water below. Madrona trees arch their vibrant red-barked limbs over the trail, and offshore an eagle may glide. Located on a bluff in West Seattle, these 130 acres of parkland offer lawns, views, beach, and water's-edge walking.

From the parking lots along Fauntleroy Way, choose any path and walk west. Wide, smooth, and graveled, they wander between large old western hemlock and Douglas fir trees. Open lawns and picnic shelters with playgrounds attract many of the park's users, but for a walk, continue west to the bluff. Sloping gently to the south, the now-paved trail gives views out onto Puget Sound and Vashon Island. Curve around and down to the shore, where fresh breezes from the south stir the water and create waves that clatter the pebbles on the beach.

Wide, paved, and level, the mile of beach walk invites either a slow stroll or a heart-pumping power walk. Winter storms bring waves that crash against the sea wall and throw mighty drift logs high on the beach. In milder weather, the shoreline begs for exploration. At the northern end, past the swimming pool, the walkway narrows to a sea wall under the branches of a slope of mixed conifers, maples and red alder. Choose a nonthreatening path up (one that slopes rather than climbs) to return to the upper park.

*How to Get There:* From I-5 south of downtown Seattle, northbound, take exit 163 (W Seattle Fwy, Columbian Way) staying left for the West Seattle Fwy. Follow it to the end and continue straight as it becomes Fauntleroy Ave SW. Curve left with Fauntleroy SW. In about 2 miles, you'll see the park on your right.

From I-5 south of downtown Seattle, southbound, take exit 163A (W Seattle Fwy, Columbian Way) onto the West Seattle Fwy and proceed as above. Seattle Parks (206) 684-4075.

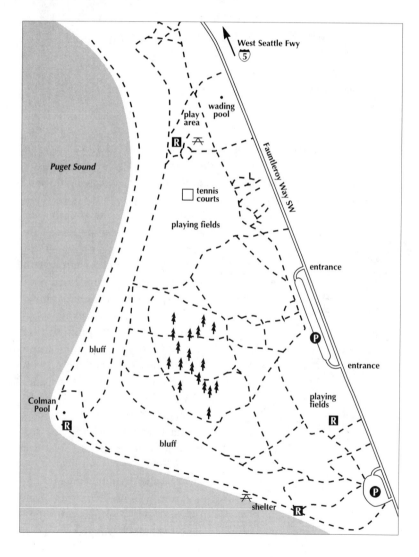

# #33
# SCHMITZ PRESERVE

**WEST SEATTLE, 5.5 MILES SOUTHWEST OF DOWNTOWN**

| | |
|---|---|
| HIGHLIGHTS | *Old growth forest, stream, bird-watching* |
| TRAIL | *0.75 mile total; natural surface* |
| OTHER USAGE | *Pedestrians only* |
| STEEPNESS | *Gentle* |
| CONNECTING TRAILS | *None* |
| PARK SERVICES | *None* |
| DISABLED ACCESS | *None* |

TO STROLL IN SCHMITZ PRESERVE IS TO SENSE HOW THE PUGET SOUND region looked before the arrival of the logging mills. Towering, massive western red cedar, western hemlock, and Douglas fir create an ancient ambience all around. Although it is not pristine—non-native English ivy

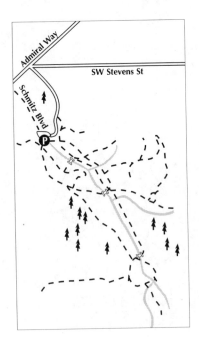

invades from the neighborhoods, and a few old stumps reveal the ravages of the logger's saw—most of the forest remains untouched. Walking the fir needle–lined path you can hear birds singing, calling, moving about, and seeking food. Listen for the tapping of the pileated woodpecker, the largest North American woodpecker, with its bright red crown, black-and-white neck, and black body. Nuthatches and brown creepers reside here, as does the less frequently seen or heard Western screech owl.

As you walk, notice the amount and variety of life that comes from fallen trees. Saplings of alder, hemlock, and Douglas fir send fine roots into the decaying wood of ancient logs. Shrubs, too, such as red huckleberry and salal, find the nutrients and moisture they need in these downed giants. Tall-standing snags house myriad insects that help supply the avian feeders. Removal of this downed wood and stumps would quickly destroy much of the life of the old forest, where the floor is often too thickly covered by needles and leaves to allow young saplings to grow.

For a more extended walk, stroll Schmitz Boulevard (closed to vehicles) out of the parking lot. This old paved road leads through a deep ravine under Admiral Way, ending at a neighborhood park and playground.

**Tree of Life:** *Native Americans had so many uses for the western red cedar that they called it the "tree of life." The wood made logs for houses and canoes and household items. From the bark they wove baskets and clothing. The needles made a natural insect repellent. The shredded bark served as diapers. Many Native Americans believed that leaning your back against the trunk infused strength.*

**How to Get There: From I-5 south of downtown Seattle, northbound, take exit 163 (W Seattle Fwy, Columbian Way) staying left to get on the West Seattle Fwy. Exit onto SW Admiral Way, following it uphill past a commercial district, then down a hill to SW Stevens St. Look on the left for the park sign just before crossing a ravine. Turn left on SW Stevens St, then bear right into the parking lot.**

**From I-5 south of downtown Seattle, southbound, take exit 163A (W Seattle Fwy, Columbian Way) onto the West Seattle Freeway and proceed as above. Seattle Parks (206) 684-4075.**

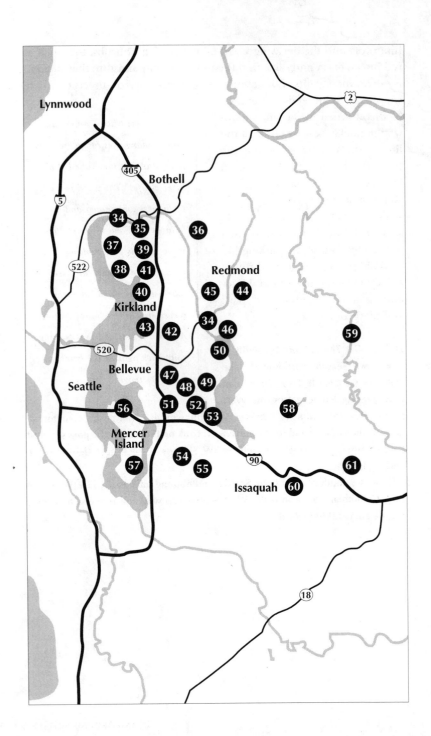

# IN AND AROUND BELLEVUE

# #34
# SAMMAMISH RIVER TRAIL

BOTHELL (11 MILES NORTH OF BELLEVUE)
TO REDMOND (6 MILES EAST OF BELLEVUE)

| | |
|---|---|
| HIGHLIGHTS | *Pastures, riverside, Cascade views, art* |
| TRAIL | *9.4 miles one way; paved* |
| OTHER USAGE | *Bicycles, horses* |
| STEEPNESS | *Level* |
| CONNECTING TRAILS | *Burke-Gilman (Walk #19), Tolt Pipeline, Puget Power/Redmond (Walk #45), Marymoor Park (Walk #46)* |
| PARK·SERVICES | *Restrooms, picnic shelters, playing fields at various parks* |
| DISABLED ACCESS | *Restrooms, trail* |

ALONG THIS RIBBON OF STILL-RURAL WASHINGTON JUST MINUTES OFF I-405 and SR 520, you'll find miles and miles of walking opportunity. Listen to the soft murmur of water, and inhale the clean air of the countryside. In Redmond the trail borders Slough House, the studio of Dudley Carter, late Artist in Residence for King County, whose huge wood sculptures can be seen both there and at nearby Marymoor Park. Slough House is usually open to the public when the front gates are open. Farther north near 124th Street, you pass close to the Chateau Ste. Michelle winery, where a free tour may lure you in from the walk.

The trail follows the grassy banks of the gently flowing Sammamish River, which connects Lake Sammamish to Lake Washington. Although surrounded to the east and west by the creeping spread of suburbia and light industry, parts of the trail still retain a rural feel.

On sunny days, the trail is host to a bevy of bicyclists, joggers, and equestrians, many of whom make the entire 9-mile jaunt between Redmond and Bothell. But at midweek, on rainy days, you're likely to find yourself talking instead to the flocks of gulls splashing in the flooded fields, or exchanging greetings with hooded mergansers in winter or the fluffy Canada goslings in spring. If the bicycle traffic alarms

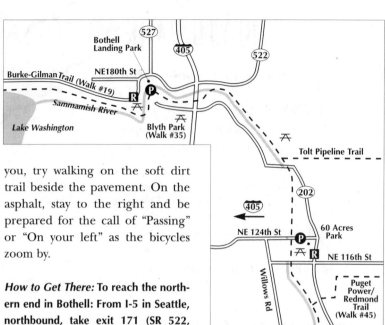

you, try walking on the soft dirt trail beside the pavement. On the asphalt, stay to the right and be prepared for the call of "Passing" or "On your left" as the bicycles zoom by.

*How to Get There:* To reach the northern end in Bothell: From I-5 in Seattle, northbound, take exit 171 (SR 522, Bothell, Lk City Way) and head north 9.3 miles. Turn right in Bothell on NE 180th St into Bothell Landing Park.

From I-5 north of Seattle, southbound, take exit 177 (SR 104, NE 205th St, Lake Forest Park). Turn left on 244th St SW and go under the freeway. Take an immediate right onto NE Ballinger Way (SR 104). Go 2.75 miles to Bothell Way NE and turn left. Go about 3.7 miles and turn right on NE 180th St into Bothell Landing Park.

From I-405 north of Bellevue, northbound, take exit 23 (SR 522 west, Bothell, Seattle). If southbound, take exit 23B (SR 522 west, Bothell). Head west on SR 522 to Bothell/Kenmore. Go about 1.6 miles and turn left on NE 180th St into Bothell Landing Park.

To reach the southern end in Redmond: Follow directions for Marymoor Park (Walk #46). Turn into Marymoor Park and you will see the paved trail to your left, before crossing the river. Park near the tennis courts (on the left) and return to the trail by paved walkways. King County Parks (206) 296-4232.

# #35
# BLYTH PARK

**BOTHELL, 13 MILES NORTH OF BELLEVUE**

| | |
|---|---|
| HIGHLIGHTS | *Lawn, forest, river* |
| TRAIL | *1 mile total; natural surface* |
| OTHER USAGE | *Pedestrians only* |
| STEEPNESS | *Steep* |
| CONNECTING TRAILS | *Tolt Pipeline (via unmaintained, rugged trail), Sammamish River Trail (Walk #34) (via footpath by river)* |
| PARK SERVICES | *Restrooms, picnic shelters, playground, trail map sign* |
| DISABLED ACCESS | *Restrooms, picnic shelters* |

A WOODED SHOULDER OF LAND FORCES THE SAMMAMISH RIVER INTO its last major turn before it makes a run for Lake Washington. Here, at the head of the lake, just minutes from both north Seattle and Bellevue, you can stroll a lawn above the river or hike the forested hillside.

A great picnic stop for the travel-weary on I-405 or for neighborhood folks wanting an outing, Blyth Park boasts a mile of steep, heart-pumping trails. A trail-map sign, courtesy of an Eagle Scout, shows the possibilities for this wooded walk. From the sign, cross the lawn past the playground to the trailhead, which is posted. The first right-hand turn puts you on the less-strenuous portion of trail, where you'll pass wooden benches as well as a picnic area nestled in a cedar grove. The trail climbs, passing several small trails made by marauding feet with no regard for potential hillside erosion. Although maintained by the city, this is no

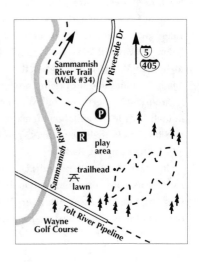

wide, gentle path; it is treacherously slippery in rain because of its clay surface and the way it clings to the hillside. On dry days, though, it offers a good workout as you ascend through the forest of conifers and deciduous trees. Two footbridges take you over a small seasonal stream, and a series of tall steps drop you back to the trailhead.

*How to Get There:* From I-5 in Seattle, northbound, take exit 171 (Rt 522, Bothell, Lake City Way) and head north for 9.8 miles. (Lake City Way NE becomes Bothell Way NE.) In Bothell, turn right on 102nd Ave NE. Cross the Sammamish River and take the first right onto W Riverside Dr. Follow it about 0.5 mile to the park entrance.

From I-5 north of Seattle, southbound, take exit 177 (SR 104, Lake Forest Park). Turn left on 244th St SW and go under the freeway. Take an immediate right onto NE Ballinger Way (SR 104) and go 2.5 miles. Turn left on Bothell Way NE and go about 4 miles. In Bothell, turn right on 102nd Ave NE and proceed as above.

From I-405 north of Bellevue, northbound, take exit 23 (SR 522 west, Bothell, Seattle). If southbound, take exit 23B (SR 522 west, Bothell). Head west on SR 522 to Bothell. Go 1 mile, turn left on 102nd Ave NE and proceed as above. Bothell Parks (206) 486-3256.

**Don't Get Carried Away:** *Rivers can change character rapidly from shallow and placid to raging, murky torrents during and after local storms or Cascade storms that increase the snow-melt. Don't walk or play along riverbanks during heavy rain or when flood warnings are in effect. Both controlled rivers (such as the Cedar, Green, and White) and free flowing rivers (such as the Snoqualmie, Stillaguamish, and Snohomish) are potentially hazardous.*

# #36
# GOLD CREEK PARK

## WOODINVILLE, 12 MILES NORTH OF BELLEVUE

| | |
|---|---|
| HIGHLIGHTS | *Stream, forest* |
| TRAIL | *2.8 miles total; natural surface* |
| OTHER USAGE | *Horses* |
| STEEPNESS | *Steep* |
| CONNECTING TRAILS | *None* |
| PARK SERVICES | *Picnic area, map sign, lodge* |
| DISABLED ACCESS | *None* |

AT FIRST GLANCE, THIS SECLUDED COUNTY PARK WITH ITS STREAM AND picnic area appears to offer nothing to a walker. But hidden behind a mantle of blackberries, a well-used trail climbs a forested ravine alongside Gold Creek.

The trail-map sign, drawn by a Boy Scout for his Eagle project, shows two loops, one north and the other south. Both begin with a steep climb up the edge of Gold Creek in quiet woods. The year-round creek gives moisture to the air, increasing the rich scent of humus and greenery. For the south loop, take the first trail to the right, as it switches back higher on the hillside. The trails in this park are used equally by walkers and horses, so they tend to be narrow, rough, and in places worn into ruts by hooves.

Rising to a ridge, you leave the forest cover for a moment to touch the edge of suburbia, and then dive back into the green shelter like that which used to cover most of the Eastside 40 or 50 years ago before the housing developments came. Now on the north loop trail, you descend past Douglas firs and western red cedars up to 2 feet in diameter. Here downed logs and open glens invite a rest or picnic.

Throughout, the trail is steep, rising and falling on the contours of the west-sloping hill. This is a great training walk, or one to challenge your children. A mossy fence marks the northern park boundary. Descend finally to the Gold Creek streambed and return to the trailhead.

In this swatch of wildness there are few landmarks, except your memory of going along the edge of a ravine or a particularly steep hillside.

Down, on any trail, should eventually return you to the trailhead.

*How to Get There:* From I-405 north of Bellevue, northbound, take exit 20B (NE 124th St). Turn right on NE 124th St. Go 2.5 miles and turn left on Hwy 202 (Woodinville-Redmond Rd NE). Go straight for 1.5 miles. At a 4-way stop go straight (the road becomes 148th Ave NE). After 0.5 mile the main road veers left, but continue straight on 148th Ave NE. The park is 0.25 mile ahead on the right.

From I-405 north of Bellevue, southbound, take exit 23A (SR 522 east to SR 202, Woodinville, Monroe) staying left to merge onto SR 522. Take the Woodinville-Redmond exit. At the end of the ramp turn right. Go straight and turn left on NE 175th St. Turn right on 140th Ave NE and go about 1.5 miles (past the Gold Creek Tennis and Racquet Club) and look for 148th Ave NE merging on the left. Take a sharp (almost U-turn) left onto 148th Ave NE and go 0.25 mile up hill to the park on the right. King County Parks (206) 296-2964.

Blackberry blossoms add sweet fragrance to Northwest forests

# #37
# SAINT EDWARD STATE PARK

### ON LAKE WASHINGTON, 13.5 MILES NORTH OF BELLEVUE

| | |
|---|---|
| HIGHLIGHTS | *Forest, ravines, lakeshore* |
| TRAIL | *7.5 miles total; natural surface, some paved* |
| OTHER USAGE | *Bicycles; horses in southeast corner* |
| STEEPNESS | *Moderate to steep* |
| CONNECTING TRAILS | *None* |
| PARK SERVICES | *Restrooms, picnic areas, playing fields, tennis and racquetball courts, swimming pool, trail map sign* |
| DISABLED ACCESS | *Restrooms, buildings, paved trail around buildings* |

DEEP RAVINES CUTTING THROUGH A FOREST OF MIXED CONIFER, MADRONA, and bigleaf maple characterize this 316-acre park, the largest piece of undeveloped property on Lake Washington. Coyotes roam the grounds in early evening, and bald eagles often nest along the shoreline. The woodlands provide shelter for many foraging and upper-canopy birds, and red-tailed hawks cruise the open edges of the meadow. Waterfowl on the lakefront include grebes, geese, and all the native ducks.

With the parking lot on a rise high above the lake, the trails in Saint Edward are among the steepest found in the region. If the narrow, leaf-strewn trails on hillsides daunt you, use the wide, gently graded Main Trail to reach the grassy "beach" on the waterfront. For more challenge, try the Gym Trail, which traverses a densely wooded hillside above a stream. Look here for white three-petalled trillium blooming in the spring. If you want to increase your aerobic exercise, return via the Grotto Trail: it's a strenuous but beautiful climb overlooking the graceful curve of a fern-draped grotto where weddings are often held.

Scattered among the hemlock, cedar, and Oregon ash, you'll see massive stumps with springboard notches cut more than 70 years ago. Look along the shoreline for rusted chains entangling many fallen trees. These are all that remain of the log boom once moored offshore.

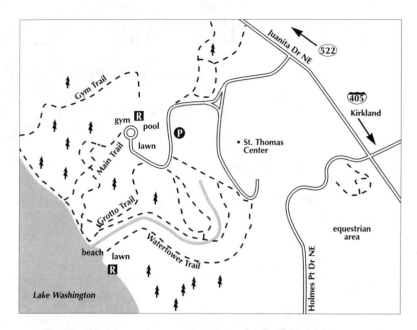

*How to Get There:* From I-405 north of Bellevue, northbound, take exit 20A (NE 116th St). Turn left on NE 116th St and go 1.5 miles to the light at 100th Ave NW. Go straight through the light onto Juanita Drive. Go about 4 miles and, at the top of the hill, look for signs on the right for the park. Turn left into the park. At the Y, bear right and go up the hill to the parking lot.

From I-405 north of Bellevue, southbound, take exit 20 (NE 124th St). Turn right at the end of the ramp and get in the left lane. Turn left at the first light onto 120th Ave NE. Turn right on NE 116th St and proceed as above.

From I-5 in Seattle, northbound, take exit 171 (SR 522, Lake City Way) and head north for 7 miles. (Lake City Way NE becomes Bothell Way NE.) In Kenmore turn right on 68th Ave NE which becomes Juanita Dr NE. Go about 2 miles and look for the park entrance on your right.

From I-5 north of Seattle, southbound, take exit 177 (SR 104, Lake Forest Park). Turn left on 244th St SW and go under the freeway. Take an immediate right onto NE Ballinger Way (SR 104). Go 2.75 miles and turn left on Bothell Way NE. Go 1.3 miles and turn right on 68th Ave NE (which becomes Juanita Dr NE) and proceed as above. Washington State Parks (206) 823-2992.

# #38
# O. O. DENNY PARK

ON LAKE WASHINGTON, 11 MILES NORTH OF BELLEVUE

| | |
|---|---|
| HIGHLIGHTS | *Beach, lakeside views, mature forest* |
| TRAIL | *1-mile loop; natural surface* |
| OTHER USAGE | *Pedestrians only; no bicycles* |
| STEEPNESS | *Moderate to steep* |
| CONNECTING TRAILS | *None* |
| PARK SERVICES | *Restrooms, picnic shelter* |
| DISABLED ACCESS | *Restrooms and beach area; not forest trail* |

FOLLOW THE CONTOURS OF A RIDGE ABOVE DENNY CREEK IN DENSE western red cedar and western hemlock stands. Sword ferns create a tufted carpet of undergrowth to hide mice, voles, and shrews. This forest of century-old trees is much as it might have been when Seattle developer O. O. Denny stepped ashore to survey the land for a homesite in the early 1900s.

On the beach side of the park, the creek has gouged an impressive ravine in its last push to the Sound. Stroll the grassy lawns, and watch for bald eagles overhead. To reach the forest trailhead, cross the road and start up the forest path to the right of the parking lot. The trail climbs steeply high above the ravine formed by the creek. At the top of the ridge, a graveled road intersects the trail. Turn around here or go left, through a small clearing past a pump house.

In summer you may see berry-rich scat lying on the ground at frequent intervals. Not cat, bear, dog, or deer. Coyote. These carnivores turn into berry eaters when other food is scarce or when berries are easy to forage. In the sunny patches on this western sloping hill the salal and blackberries are abundant.

Near the old pump house find a narrow path descending into the Denny Creek ravine and back. This section of trail is narrower and in summer is lined with nettles. Marvelous cedar and Douglas fir stumps hint at the past majesty of this forest. If the trail is too overgrown, return to the parking lot via the ridge trail. Members of the Denny Creek Association patrol this precious enclave of old forest and ask visiting walkers to respect the land and the trails.

Sword ferns carpet the forest floor creating shelter for small woodland creatures

*How to Get There:* From I-405 north of Bellevue, northbound, take exit 20A (NE 116th St) and turn left on NE 116th St. Go 1.4 miles to the light at 100th Ave NW. Go straight through the light onto Juanita Dr NE. Go another 2 miles and turn left on 76th Ave NE (which becomes Holmes Point Dr NE). Look for the park in about 1 more mile.

From I-405 north of Bellevue, southbound, take exit 20 (NE 124th St). Turn right at the end of the ramp and get in the left lane. Turn left at the first light onto 120th Ave NE. Turn right on NE 116th St and proceed as above.

From I-5 in Seattle, northbound, take exit 171 (SR 522, Bothell, Lake City Way) and head north for 7 miles. (Lake City Way NE becomes Bothell Way NE.) In Kenmore, turn right on 68th Ave NE (which becomes Juanita Dr NE). Go about 2 miles and turn right on Holmes Point Dr NE. Go another 2 miles to the park.

From I-5 north of Seattle, southbound, take exit 177 (SR 104, Lake Forest park). Turn left on 244th St SW and go under the freeway. Take an immediate right onto NE Ballinger Way (SR 104). Go 2.75 miles and turn left on Bothell Way NE. Go 1.3 miles and turn right on 68th Ave NE (which becomes Juanita Dr NE), and proceed as above.

Parking lots are on both sides of the road. King County Parks (206) 296-4232.

# #39
# EDITH MOULTON PARK

### 9 MILES NORTH OF BELLEVUE

| | |
|---|---|
| HIGHLIGHTS | *Mature forest, historical site* |
| TRAIL | *1.4-mile loop and spurs; paved in meadow, natural in forest* |
| OTHER USAGE | *Bicycles on paved trail (use in forest is being evaluated and may change)* |
| STEEPNESS | *Level to gentle* |
| CONNECTING TRAILS | *None* |
| PARK SERVICES | *Picnic shelter, benches* |
| DISABLED ACCESS | *Paved meadow trail* |

IT IS WITH A SENSE OF WONDER THAT YOU STEP UPON THE FOREST PATH of this small, almost secret place in the Juanita district of Kirkland. Here stand the same cedar and Douglas fir of a century ago. Which ones, you might wonder, did young Edith Moulton, who grew up here at the turn of the century, hide behind while playing hide-and-seek with her friends? Did she sit on her long skirts on the bank of Juanita Creek and watch the salmon returning each fall? And did she, too, watch the hairy woodpeckers hop up the cottonwood trunks?

This tiny park, just 26 acres, is a microcosm of the best of today's Northwest forests. Walk slowly on soft dirt trails under huge hemlocks, cedars, and firs. Find dry footing on a wooden bridge over clear and bubbling Juanita Creek. Sit on a huge downed log and watch the squirrels play in the alders. Explore narrow trails that dead-end in thickets or bring you round to rejoin the main trail.

Edith Moulton was born in 1897 and was raised by her grandmother in an old farmhouse on this land. After attending the University of

Washington, she taught school on the Olympic Peninsula and then returned to Juanita to live out the rest of her life. In 1962 she bequeathed her homestead to the county, saying, "We must save some nature spots for posterity before it is too late."

This one is worth a stop if you're passing by on I-405 and need a leg stretch or a lawn for a picnic, or if you just want to see what Juanita used to look like.

*How to Get There:* **From I-405 north of Bellevue, northbound, take exit 20B (NE 124th St). Turn left on NE 124th St and go over the freeway. Take the first right onto 116th Ave NE. Turn left at the light at NE 132nd St, then right at the light on 108th Ave NE. The park is on the right at the corner of NE 137th Pl. Park on the street by the Meadow Entrance with its historical information sign.**

**From I-405 north of Bellevue, southbound, take exit 20 (NE 124th St) and turn right at the end of the ramp. Take the next right onto 116th Ave NE and proceed as above. King County Parks (206) 296-4232.**

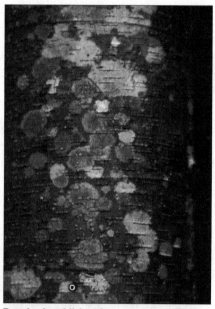

Pastel-colored lichen form patterns on the smooth bark of alders

# #40
# JUANITA BAY PARK

**KIRKLAND, ON LAKE WASHINGTON, 8 MILES NORTH OF BELLEVUE**

| | |
|---|---|
| HIGHLIGHTS | *Wetlands, lake views, bird-watching* |
| TRAIL | *1.3 miles; paved and boardwalk* |
| OTHER USAGE | *Bicycles* |
| STEEPNESS | *Level to gentle* |
| CONNECTING TRAILS | *None* |
| PARK SERVICES | *Restrooms, picnic tables, interpretive signs* |
| DISABLED ACCESS | *Restrooms, all trails* |

AN APRON OF GREEN LAWN SPREADS OUT FROM THE STREETS OF SUBURBIA, creating an elegant separation between the manmade and the natural. Below the lawns, hidden from casual view, are boardwalks that meander into natural marshes where blackbirds nest, frogs sun and leap, and cattails sway in lakeside breezes.

**Picnickers enjoy a clear day near the wetlands at Juanita Bay Park**

This corner of Lake Washington has had a long and active past. Native Americans gathered food here on the shores of the once-higher lake. Later came the frog farmers and the truck gardeners, both working with the land and lake as it was. In 1932 a Kirkland realtor began an onslaught against nature by dumping thousands of truckloads of cedar bark, sawdust, and dirt to fill the marshes and build a golf course. But the inexorable water won out and, despite berms and pumps, the course was finally closed in 1975.

Slowly, now, the lake reclaims its shaggy marsh shoreline. You can observe this wetland either from the broad paved causeway on the eastern edge of the lake or from the boardwalks that wend their ways into the thickets of cattails and reeds. Here you may see mallards and teals dabbling, mergansers diving, or beavers gliding across their carefully crafted ponds.

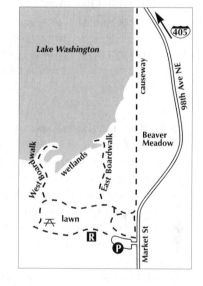

*How to Get There:* **From I-405 north of Bellevue, northbound, take exit 20A (NE 116th St). Turn left and go about 1.5 miles. Turn left (south) on 98th Ave NE which becomes Market St and borders the park. Turn right into the parking lot.**

**From I-405 north of Bellevue, southbound, take exit 20 (NE 124th St). Turn right at the end of the ramp and get in the left lane. Turn left at the first light onto 120th Ave NE to parallel the freeway. Turn right on NE 116th St and proceed as above. Kirkland Parks (206) 828-1217.**

# #41
# CRESTWOODS PARK

## KIRKLAND, 8 MILES NORTH OF BELLEVUE

| | |
|---|---|
| HIGHLIGHTS | *Lawn, young deciduous forest* |
| TRAIL | *1.1 miles total; paved and natural surfaces* |
| OTHER USAGE | *Bicycles* |
| STEEPNESS | *Gentle to steep* |
| CONNECTING TRAILS | *None* |
| PARK SERVICES | *Restrooms, picnic tables, playing fields, playground* |
| DISABLED ACCESS | *Restrooms, playing field areas via paved trails; not forest trails* |

THE ASPHALT WALKWAYS AROUND LANDSCAPED LAWNS AT CRESTWOODS Park are perfect for wet-weather walking, but on drier days the true charm of this neighborhood park is found in the forest beyond them. The changing seasons enhance the beauty of the immature red alder, vine maple, and bigleaf maple. Soft summer breezes rustle the leaves, fall color delights the eyes, and winter branches are stenciled sharply against the sky. The undergrowth of blackberry brings heady scents with spring blossoms and luscious snacks for late-summer walkers.

Narrow but well-used dirt trails lead from the soccer fields, from behind the baseball diamond, and along the southern boundary. From the soccer fields, the trail winds through high blackberry gently down a slope to meet the main north-south trail. Follow it north past spur trails that overlook the Burlington Northern railroad, on which trains still roar by several times per day. At the fence, turn back south, parallel to the tracks. A few mature cedars and bigleaf maples stand in contrast to the younger trees, and the more heavily shaded areas have won against blackberry to welcome ferns. A spur trail at the southern end takes you across the tracks and up erosion-control stairs made from, appropriately, railroad ties. Another spur trail leaves from the paved walkway by the soccer fields and drops steeply down more railroad ties to Forbes Creek Drive. The two spurs make great training stair climbs.

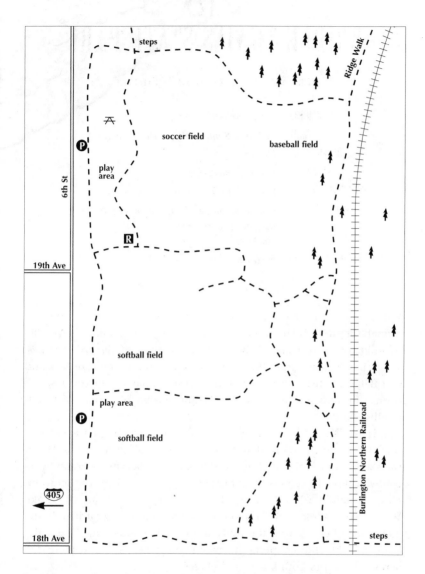

*How to Get There:* From I-405 north of Bellevue, north- or southbound, take exit 18 (SR 908, NE 85th St, Kirkland, Redmond) and head west (left turn if northbound, right turn if southbound). Go about 0.5 mile and turn right on 6th St at the light. Follow 6th St until it curves and becomes 15th Ave. Turn right on 5th Pl. Go up the hill and turn right on 18th St to the park. Kirkland Parks (206) 828-1217.

# #42
# BRIDLE TRAILS STATE PARK

KIRKLAND, 5.5 MILES NORTH OF BELLEVUE

| | |
|---|---|
| HIGHLIGHTS | *Forest, equestrian activities* |
| TRAIL | *At least 28 miles total; natural surface* |
| OTHER USAGE | *Horses* |
| STEEPNESS | *Gentle to moderate* |
| CONNECTING TRAILS | *Bridle Crest Trail (many road crossings)* |
| PARK SERVICES | *Restrooms, picnic area, arena, stands, show ring, horse shows, posted map, brochures* |
| DISABLED ACCESS | *Restroom, picnic area* |

YOU MAY NOT SEE THE DOUGLAS SQUIRRELS CHOMP ON FIR CONES AS though they were corn on the cob, but walking through this almost 100-year-old forest, you are likely to see many piles of discarded scales. Though only a mile from the freeway and the urban centers of Kirkland and Bellevue, this enclave of mature forest is a habitat for coyotes, raccoons, possums, the native squirrels, and dozens of species of forest-dwelling birds.

It is like home, too, to many horseback riders, who regularly exercise their steeds on the more than 28 miles of natural-surface trails. When the state acquired the land in the 1930s, it soon became overrun by locals who thought of it as their private drag strip for cars and motorcycles. A neighborhood group formed, later becoming the Lake Washington Saddle Club, and took on the role of forest guardian. In the 1940s, members cleared the trails and built the show ring. Today the State and the club cooperate in maintaining the park, and these 480 acres are open to both hikers and horses.

Entering by the big arena on 116th Avenue NE, take the trail heading up the gentle hill to the east, which quickly puts you under canopies of fir and hemlock that soon muffle the freeway noise. After a good rain, you'll find a few deep mudholes, so wear appropriate shoes. If the weather has been dry, you can probably negotiate the edges of the mire without mishap.

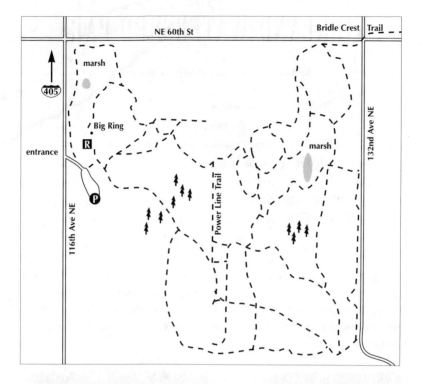

Bridle Trails is a great walk for those who know or want to get to know the indigenous plants. Here you'll find several varieties of ferns, Oregon grape, huckleberry, salal, and many species of wild mushrooms, some edible and others poisonous.

With miles of interweaving trails, it's easy to become disoriented. The western part of the park is the most straightforward. Trails east of the power lines meander like a child's scribbles. If you feel lost, just ask someone. All the riders know their way around, and are receptive to friendly hikers.

***How to Get There:*** **From I-405 north of Bellevue, north- or southbound, take exit 17 (NE 70th Pl). If northbound, turn right at the end of the ramp onto 116th Ave NE and go about 1 mile to the park entrance on your left. If southbound, turn right at the end of the ramp, cross the freeway, then turn right again onto 116th Ave NE and go about 1 mile to the park entrance. Park at the northeast corner to access trails. Washington State Parks: Lake Sammamish Office (206) 455-7010.**

# #43
# KIRKLAND WATERSHED PARK

### KIRKLAND, 3.5 MILES NORTH OF BELLEVUE

| | |
|---|---|
| HIGHLIGHTS | *Forest, stream* |
| TRAIL | *2.8 miles total; natural surface* |
| OTHER USAGE | *Bicycles (pedestrians only preferred)* |
| STEEPNESS | *Gentle to steep* |
| CONNECTING TRAILS | *None* |
| PARK SERVICES | *None* |
| DISABLED ACCESS | *None* |

SUNLIGHT TRACES DANCING PICTURES ON THE PATH. BIRD CALLS AND songs lilt from one tree to another. Mount Rainier stands tall above a valley of yellow Scotch broom. A clear pool quenches the thirst of a family of coyotes. And all of this is just minutes from both Kirkland and Bellevue.

A small sanctuary of second-growth forest near downtown Kirkland

From the 1930s to the late 1960s a small reservoir in the watershed was built to supply Kirkland's water needs, but the system had too many leaks, and in 1967 Kirkland hooked up with Seattle for water. Today all that remain of this human effort are an empty reservoir and a few pipes partially buried beneath bracken and sword ferns.

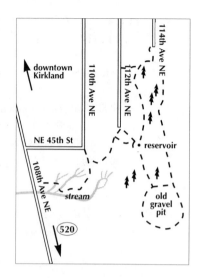

For easy walking, follow the chip-lined paths in a loop at the eastern edge of the forest, where rufous-sided towhees and Bewick's wrens hop about on the forest floor and in the branches of the madrona and maple trees. At the southern end you come to a ridge above a Scotch broom–filled valley, carved out 30 years ago for gravel to build I-405. A sandy footpath that dips down into the valley makes another appealing walking loop.

From the 112th Avenue entrance a steep but well-maintained trail heads west, sloping down and around old stumps and seedling–covered nurse logs. Follow the path into the ravine. Here, less freeway noise intrudes on the forest sounds, and soon the sound of the stream dominates. In the quiet, clear pool, shadows of minnows pattern the sandy bottom.

***How to Get There:*** From I-5 in Seattle, north- or southbound, take exit 168B (SR 520, Bellevue) across Lake Washington. Take the Kirkland (Lake Washington Blvd NE) exit. Turn left at the end of the ramp, cross the freeway, and turn right on Northup Way. At the next light, turn left on 108th Ave NE. Go about 1 mile and turn right on NE 45th St or NE 53rd St, then right on 110th Ave NE, 112th Ave NE, or 114th Ave NE for on-street parking.

From I-405 in Bellevue, north- or southbound, take exit 14 (SR 520) west, and exit immediately onto 108th Ave NE. Go about 1 mile north and proceed as above. Kirkland Parks (206) 828-1217.

# #44
# FARREL-McWHIRTER PARK

### REDMOND, 10 MILES NORTHEAST OF BELLEVUE

| | |
|---|---|
| HIGHLIGHTS | *Farm animals, forest, salmon-spawning stream* |
| TRAIL | *2 miles total; paved and natural surfaces* |
| OTHER USAGE | *Bicycles on paved surfaces, horses on designated trails only* |
| STEEPNESS | *Level to gentle* |
| CONNECTING TRAILS | *Puget Power/ Redmond Trail (Walk #45)* |
| PARK SERVICES | *Restrooms, picnic shelters, playground, horse arena, classes* |
| DISABLED ACCESS | *Restrooms (via gravel area), buildings, paved trail* |

BEYOND THE SEDUCTIVE GREEN LAWN, THE PICNIC AREA, AND THE clucking, oinking, and bleating farm animals lies an inviting swath of mature (80-year-old) forest. Wide, natural trails form a loop inside the park for walkers, while horseback riders are confined to the outer trail and arena area.

Cool, shallow Mackey Creek bisects the park—open spaces to the south, forest to the north. In summer, day campers study the flora and fauna of the forest and stream habitat and learn to care for the rabbits, goats, pigs, ponies, ducks, and chickens. Thousands of children may know these trails better than their parents.

To explore the forest, bid adieu to the animals and head north on paved Charlotte's Trail, then turn right into the forest on the wide, soft-surfaced path. For a short time, leave civilization behind as you wander under stately Douglas fir and inhale the spicy scent of western red cedar. Let your eyes rove over the lacy green carpet of ladyferns and sword ferns. In spring, orange and yellow salmonberries and white trillium punctuate the lush greenery, and white blackberry flowers promise sweet fruits for summer. Look for evidence of deer, and listen for the shriek of the red-tailed hawk high overhead.

*How to Get There:* From I-5 in Seattle, north- or southbound, take exit 168B (SR 520, Bellevue) across Lake Washington and continue east on SR 520 to its end at Avondale Rd. Go about 1 mile north on Avondale Rd and turn right on Novelty Hill Rd. Go .25 mile and turn left on Redmond Rd (signposted). Go 0.5 mile and turn left into the park.

From I-405 in Bellevue, north- or southbound, take exit 14 (SR 520, Redmond) east to the end of SR 520 and proceed as above. Redmond Parks (206) 556-2300.

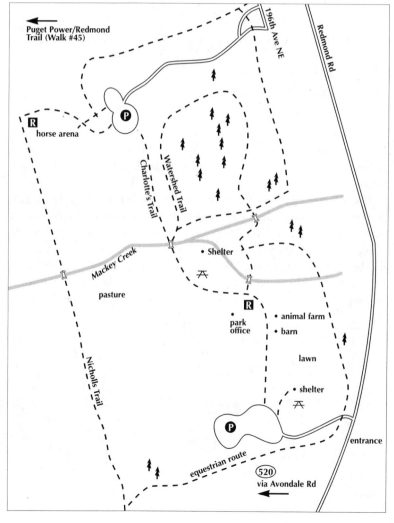

# 45

# PUGET POWER/REDMOND TRAIL

### REDMOND, 10 MILES NORTHEAST OF BELLEVUE

| | |
|---|---|
| HIGHLIGHTS | *Rolling hills, Cascade views, meadow, forest* |
| TRAIL | *3 miles one way; gravel and natural surfaces* |
| OTHER USAGE | *Bicycles, horses* |
| STEEPNESS | *Gentle to steep* |
| CONNECTING TRAILS | *Links Sammamish River Trail (Walk #34) to Farrel-McWhirter Park (Walk #44)* |
| PARK SERVICES | *None* |
| DISABLED ACCESS | *None* |

JUST NORTH OF DOWNTOWN REDMOND, THIS RUGGED STRETCH OF GREEN space is appealing for its ups and downs, bushes alive with birds, and striking views of the Cascades.

If walking under power lines is not your idea of fun, forget this trail. But perhaps you can play mental games to imagine these towering structures as some sort of 1950s War of the Worlds creatures, or go into engineering bliss imaging the equations necessary to erect them. Or maybe, like the wildlife that frequents these corridors of steel and wire, you can ignore them. Look for scat along the trail and telltale footprints in mud. As for larger mammals, this corridor that stretches from the

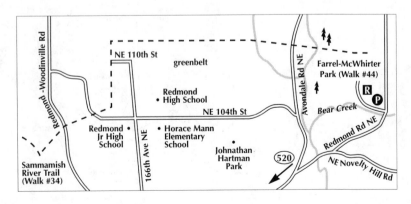

Redmond watershed to the Sammamish River boasts coyotes, raccoons, possum, deer, and lynx.

The trail varies in its surroundings, sometimes following country roads, at other times bordering neighborhoods and backyards. There are several street crossings: be cautious at the Redmond-Woodinville Road, which has only a flashing light. For much of the trail you walk in a narrow greenbelt of Scotch broom, blackberry, salmonberry, and horsetail. (Sometimes real horse tails, too, as you pass the fence of a friendly equine.) After crossing Avondale Road (with a light), the trail, at its eastern end, enters quiet second-growth forest, where evidence of long-ago logging shows in springboard slots on the moss-covered stumps. This is the more peaceful, magical end of the trail, with a soft fir-needled path underfoot, a bridge over Bear Creek, and in spring, the pinkish floral bells of salal. The trail currently ends at Farrel-McWhirter Park (Walk #44).

Where you turn around depends on your time and mood. The trail is great for power walks and training, but also for quiet contemplation. You might decide to set your sights on a certain street crossing. But be warned, there's always the lure of another Cascade view to draw you onward.

*How to Get There:* **At the western end, the trail is accessible only from the Sammamish River Trail (Walk #34). The Puget Power/Redmond Trail meets the Sammamish River Trail between Sixty Acres Park (off NE 116th St) and downtown Redmond (off NE 85th St near the city offices).**

**To reach Sixty Acres Park: From I-405 north of Bellevue, northbound, take exit 20 (NE 124th St). If southbound, take exit 20B (NE 124th St). Go east on NE 124th St about 1.5 miles and turn right on Willow Rd NE. Go 1.5 miles and turn left on NE 116th St to the Sammamish River Trail. Walk south on the Sammamish River Trail looking for the sign to the Puget Power/Redmond Trail (under the power lines.)**

**There is ample parking where the eastern end of the Puget Power/Redmond trail adjoins Farrel-McWhirter Park (Walk #44). Redmond Parks (206) 556-2300.**

# #46
# MARYMOOR PARK

### REDMOND, NORTH SHORE OF LAKE SAMMAMISH,
### 7.5 MILES NORTHEAST OF BELLEVUE

| | |
|---|---|
| HIGHLIGHTS | *River, wetlands, off-leash area, meadows, nature trail, art, historical site* |
| TRAIL | *5 miles total; paved and natural surfaces* |
| OTHER USAGE | *Bicycles, horses on equestrian trail only* |
| STEEPNESS | *Level* |
| CONNECTING TRAILS | *Sammamish River Trail (Walk #34), Bridle Trails State Park (Walk #42), via Bridle Crest Trail* |
| PARK SERVICES | *Restrooms, picnic shelters, tennis courts, playing fields, museum, bicycle velodrome, model airplane field, pea patch, climbing rock* |
| DISABLED ACCESS | *Restrooms, some trails and picnic areas, but not the southern riverside walk.* |

MARYMOOR'S VAST, OPEN SPACES—520 ACRES OF THEM—GIVE THIS park a true year-round appeal. Walkers can chose to watch the bicyclists careen around the sloped velodrome or gape at the non-acrophobic at-

tacking tiny handholds on the climbing rock. An undulating whine and hum comes from the eastern edge of the park, where land-bound pilots put their model airplanes through their tricks.

For a more serene walk, take the nature trail south into the alder and oak forest. Interpretive signs guide you along a boardwalk over a peat bog, then out to the northern shore of Lake Sammamish. Completing the loop, the boardwalk leads back along the Sammamish River through

**Windmill at snow-dusted Marymoor**

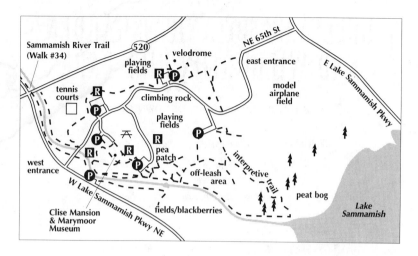

a thicket of blackberries and salal and the gentle shade of alders. Here songbirds chatter and flit, and on the river you can see the iridescent flash of the mallard drakes or the elegant suits of the Canada geese.

Where the boardwalk ends, be prepared to greet the dogs. Hundreds of them. Marymoor's off-leash area is a mecca for dogs, where they can romp and dig on the water's edge and in the fragrant fields adjoining.

Year-round, keep the binoculars handy for a look at the red-tailed hawks circling overhead. On hot summer days, expect a sky alive with hot-air balloons as they glide to rest on Marymoor's fields. Bring a camera, and flex your muscles if you want to help deflate the billowing nylon.

What is now the park was developed in the early 1900s as a family cattle farm. The original Willowmoor farmers used to boat across Lake Washington and then drive buckboards to the stately entrance of the farm. The old farmhouse remains, now a museum, as do the remnants of the drive and the bridge across the river. Inside, the museum takes you back to a time when the Eastside was a wild and rugged place.

**How to Get There:** From I-5 in Seattle, north- or southbound, take exit 168B (SR 520, Bellevue) across Lake Washington. Pass the I-405 interchange and continue east on SR 520 another 4.8 miles to the W Lake Sammamish Pkwy exit (signposted for Marymoor Park). At the end of the ramp go right on W Lake Sammamish Pkwy, then immediately left at the next light into the park.

From I-405 in Bellevue, north- or southbound, take exit 14 (SR 520, Redmond) east. Proceed as above. King County Parks (206) 296-4232.

# #47
# BELLEVUE BOTANICAL GARDEN AND WILBURTON HILL PARK

**BELLEVUE, 2.5 MILES EAST OF DOWNTOWN**

| | |
|---|---|
| HIGHLIGHTS | *Botanical garden, Japanese Garden, forest* |
| TRAIL | *Over 3 miles total; paved, gravel, and natural surfaces* |
| OTHER USAGE | *Pedestrians only in garden; dogs and bicycles in Wilburton Hill Park* |
| STEEPNESS | *Gentle* |
| CONNECTING TRAILS | *Kelsey Creek Park (Walk #48), via streets on Lake-to-Lake Trail* |
| PARK SERVICES | *Restrooms, horticultural classes, concerts, gift shop, picnic tables, playground, playing fields, tennis courts* |
| DISABLED ACCESS | *Restrooms, Botanical Garden loop* |

ALTHOUGH BELLEVUE BOTANICAL GARDEN IS TECHNICALLY WITHIN the borders of Wilburton Hill Park, the two are very different places. In Wilburton, beyond the playing fields, you walk through a forest green with salal and Douglas fir; in the Garden, you are led along established paths showcasing native and hybrid plants and vibrant floral displays.

For a good warm-up walk, head east from the Wilburton parking lot to the loop trail that borders the playing fields. As you enter the forest, it becomes a richly scented wood-chip trail zigzagging to the eastern boundary. Here, turn left along the quiet residential street for part of a block, then head back into the forest on a smaller, woodsy spur trail. Near the playing fields, you pass an innovative playground, where kids can scramble up and down the spider web and frolic in and out of the "town hall."

When you're ready for a quieter, slower stroll, step into the manicured year-round symphony of color in the Botanical Garden.

The original owners, Cal and Harriet Shorts, toiled for many years to transform the heavy clay soil into the rich loam of the garden, and the work continues. Two years after the City of Bellevue received the land as a donation, the garden opened with 36 acres of woodlands, gardens, bogs, and meadows. Today it is a showplace for the Northwest Perennial Alliance, the Eastside Fuchsia Society, the King County Herb Society, and the American Rock Garden Society.

Follow the graveled Garden Loop Trail into a glory of huge rhododendrons set in a forest of hemlock and fir. The Yao Garden is a contemporary garden that combines both Japanese and Northwest influences. Along the western slope of the garden, the Perennial Border, already world-famous, is reminiscent of an abstract painting created with plants, each carefully chosen for the hue and shape of both flower and foliage.

*How to Get There:* From I-405 in Bellevue, northbound, take exit 13B (NE 8th St). Turn right onto NE 8th St and go about 0.6 mile. Turn right (south) on 124th St NE and follow it until it makes a sharp right and becomes Main St. Wilburton Park is straight ahead. The Garden entrance is to the right on Main St.

From I-405 in Bellevue, southbound, take exit 13B (NE 8th St). Turn left onto NE 8th St and proceed as above.

For information on docent-led garden tours, the gift shop, or classes, call the Botanical Garden (206) 451-3755. Bellevue Parks (206) 455-6881.

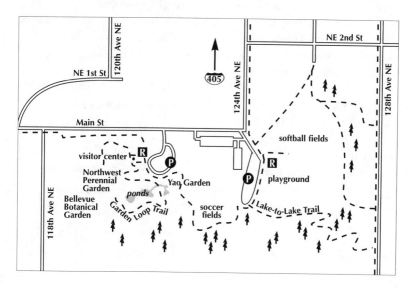

# #48

# KELSEY CREEK PARK

BELLEVUE, 3 MILES EAST OF DOWNTOWN

| | |
|---|---|
| HIGHLIGHTS | *Farm animals, pasture, forest, salmon-spawning creek* |
| TRAIL | *2.5 miles of loops and spurs; gravel and natural surfaces* |
| OTHER USAGE | *Bicycles on gravel; pedestrians only on forest trail* |
| STEEPNESS | *Gentle to steep* |
| CONNECTING TRAILS | *Lake-to-Lake Trail (via streets)* |
| PARK SERVICES | *Restrooms, picnic tables, farm animals, classes, historic cabin* |
| DISABLED ACCESS | *Restrooms, farm* |

TUCKED NEATLY INTO A NOOK OF SUBURBAN BELLEVUE, THIS WELL-loved park surprises newcomers with open meadows and fenced pastures, the baa-ing of sheep and the clucking of chickens.

This early 1900s–style farm with its white fences, red barns, pens of pigs, and peacocks has long been a favorite with families wanting to show their children how farm animals were raised before the advent of chicken factories. From the parking lot, cross a tributary of Kelsey Creek to lawns, picnic areas, and a small marsh with wild ducks. Then climb the hill to the barnyard. A graveled loop road takes you past the ducks and ponies, then to the south by the old pioneer log cabin, moved here for renovation and preservation.

Most visitors end their tour here, returning to picnic by the

**What Is That?** *Find out by joining a naturalist-led walk. Most are free. Call your city or county parks department for information. Parks also offer classes in outdoor-related topics such as gardening, birding, geology, animal care, naturalist studies, and science. Fees may apply.*

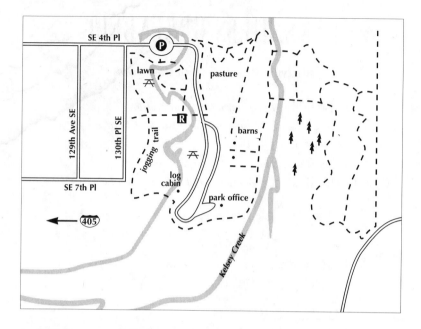

stream. But east of the barns and pony fields, another trail follows the pasture edge and then dives into the wooded hillside at the footbridge over Kelsey Creek. Here several adjoining loops take you up soft, needle-lined paths, over footbridges above marshes. Wooden steps take you higher into the deciduous forest where, in fall, the red and yellow leaves of the maples frame the farm buildings below, and in winter the vista opens to show a broad expanse of this farmland park. In spring look for the white hanging flowers, and in summer the red berries of the Indian plum.

*How to Get There:* From I-405 in Bellevue, north- or southbound, take exit 12 (SE 8th St). Go east (right if northbound, left if southbound) on SE 8th St. Go under the railroad trestle to the light at Lake Hills Connector. Go straight onto SE 7th Pl. Go a few blocks and turn left on 130th Ave SE, and then right on SE 4th Pl into the park. Bellevue Parks (206) 455-6881.

# #49
# LAKE HILLS GREENBELT

**BELLEVUE, 3.5 MILES EAST OF DOWNTOWN**

| | |
|---|---|
| HIGHLIGHTS | *Lakes, farm land, bird-watching* |
| TRAIL | *1.75 miles one way; paved and gravel* |
| OTHER USAGE | *Bicycles* |
| STEEPNESS | *Level* |
| CONNECTING TRAILS | *Lake-to-Lake Trail and Phantom Lake Trail (via streets)* |
| PARK SERVICES | *Restrooms, ranger station, display garden, classes, free nature walks late spring through September* |
| DISABLED ACCESS | *Restrooms, ranger station, some trail sections* |

IF YOU BEGIN YOUR WALK AT THE LARSEN LAKE BLUEBERRY FARM, you may see a single great blue heron standing in motionless, graceful posture among the lakeshore reeds, watching for fish, frogs, salamanders, and other aquatic prey. Ripples on the water tell of diving ducks, and between the water-lily pads iridescent male mallards and their quacking brown mates glide. Both Larsen and Phantom Lakes, at the two ends of the Lake Hills Greenbelt, are important stopovers for waterfowl along the Pacific Flyway. As many as 24 species have been identified, including green-winged teals, Northern shovelers, and ruddy ducks.

In the twigs of the 40-year-old blueberry bushes, wrens and sparrows flit and twitter. In late summer look for flocks of cedar waxwings feeding on the berries.

Continuing around Larsen Lake, the trail turns east then south along the reed-lined irrigation channel, crosses Lake Hills Boulevard (there's a crosswalk with a flashing light), and then enters an open meadow rimmed by conifers—good hunting grounds for red-tailed, Cooper's, and sharp-shinned hawks. In the forest of Douglas fir and Sitka spruce, watch for signs of squirrels and the more secretive coyotes that travel the game trails through the undergrowth. River otters have been spotted in the lakes and the stream, as well as moles and muskrats.

At the corner of SE 16th Street and 156th Avenue SE a small fruit stand operates through fall, selling fresh produce harvested from the rich peat-bog soils of the neighboring farms. If you turn west here, along SE 16th Street, you come immediately to the Display Garden, where you can pore over informative signs about a variety of herbs, flowers, and produce and investigate a "hands-on" display of composting techniques. At the Lake Hills Greenbelt Ranger Station, adjoining the garden, you'll find dioramas of the wildlife of the Greenbelt, and a three-dimensional display of the Larsen/Phantom Lake drainage.

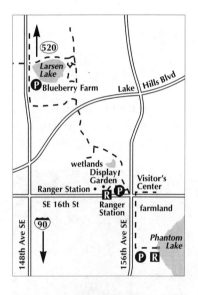

Members of the East Lake Chapter of the Audubon Society often staff a booth to answer questions about the area's birds. Cross 156th Avenue SE diagonally to continue another quarter mile to the dock and boat launch on Phantom Lake.

*How to Get There:* From I-405 in Bellevue, north- or southbound, take exit 14 (SR 520, Redmond) east. Take the 148th Ave NE exit, south. Turn right on 148th Ave NE and go 2.2 miles to the light at SE 8th St. Smaller vehicles can make a U-turn (on the green left turn arrow) and go north 1 block to park in the Greenbelt parking lot by the blueberry farm. Alternatively, to park at the Ranger Station, continue south another 0.5 mile on 148th Ave SE and turn left (east) on SE 16th St. Continue for another 0.5 mile and park at the corner of 156th Ave SE.

From I-90 east of Lake Washington, eastbound, take exit 11B (148th Ave SE) and go north on 148th Ave SE to the blueberry farm parking lot north of SE 8th. OR, turn right on SE 16th St and look for the Ranger Station just before 156th Ave SE. Greenbelt Ranger Station (206) 451-7225. Bellevue Parks (206) 455-6881.

# #50
# ARDMORE TRAILS

BELLEVUE, 5.5 MILES EAST OF DOWNTOWN

|  |  |
|---|---|
| HIGHLIGHTS | *Forest* |
| TRAIL | *1.5 miles with spurs; natural surface* |
| OTHER USAGE | *Pedestrians only* |
| STEEPNESS | *Gentle to moderate* |
| CONNECTING TRAILS | *None* |
| PARK SERVICES | *None* |
| DISABLED ACCESS | *None* |

THIS COMPACT NEIGHBORHOOD PARK IS A WALKER'S DREAM, WITH WIDE, wood-chip trails through a spacious forest of hemlock, cedar, and Douglas fir. Although it's nestled in the heart of suburbia, its sounds are

**Fern-draped ravine at Ardmore Trails**

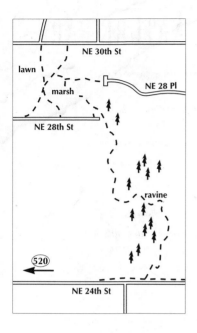

sylvan, not motorized. In summer, robins hop along the trail and chickadees and wrens call from the branches.

The trail meanders up and down gentle terrain and along the sides of a ravine cut by a tiny stream, where bare earth on the sides tells of winter flooding. So open is the forest floor, the path gives the impression of even greater length than its true 1.5 miles. The spacious forest and the silence are so compelling you could wish the trail went on and on through these sword-fern valleys and hills.

Summer visitors are rewarded with a feast of blackberries, red huckleberries, and thimbleberries. Traversing from south to north, you cross a bridge and angle up a short, steep hill some local walkers call "cardiac hill." An untrustworthy-looking rope swing dangles above a ravine, and moss-covered steps tell of once-loved tree houses built long ago by neighborhood kids.

The trail leads to a marshy patch of skunk cabbage in a cedar glen, but a sturdy puncheon bridge keeps your feet dry in this dell of old tree stumps. Here signposts point to several different park exits, each only a tenth of a mile away.

On the northwest corner lies the tiny lawn, perfect for picnics (although there are no tables or other amenities) either before or after this charming walk.

***How to Get There:*** From I-405 in Bellevue, north- or southbound, take exit 14 (SR 520, Redmond) east. Take the 148th Ave NE exit, south. Turn right on 148th Ave NE then left immediately on NE 24th St. Go about 1.5 miles and look on the left for the "Nature Trail" sign and entrance. Other entrances are located on suburban streets as shown on the map. The picnic lawn lies along NE 30th St. Parking is on streets and limited. Bellevue Parks (206) 455-6881.

# #51

# MERCER SLOUGH NATURE PARK

BELLEVUE, 2.5 MILES SOUTH OF DOWNTOWN

| | |
|---|---|
| HIGHLIGHTS | *Freshwater slough, wetlands, bird-watching, historical site* |
| TRAIL | *6 miles; paved and natural surfaces* |
| OTHER USAGE | *Bicycles on paved trails (bicycle use discouraged on soft-surface trails)* |
| STEEPNESS | *Level to gentle* |
| CONNECTING TRAILS | *Lake-to-Lake Trail (via streets)* |
| PARK SERVICES | *Restrooms, interpretive center, museum, classes, brochures, interpretive trail* |
| DISABLED ACCESS | *Restrooms; paved trail along Bellevue Way, I-90, and 118th Avenue SE* |

JUST MINUTES FROM DOWNTOWN BELLEVUE, YOU CAN STROLL MILES OF secluded trails that surround the Mercer Slough and wetlands, a paradise for birds and bird-watchers alike. Here, in fall and spring, thousands of migrating waterfowl on the Pacific Flyway en route to and from the Arctic find vital haven. Many stay over for the winter, making their nests in the cattails and reeds along the edges of the slough. Not only a haven for waterfowl, the surrounding iris and cattail marsh, blackberry thickets, and cottonwood trees provide habitat for more than a hundred other species of birds, including eagles, pheasant, owls, swifts, thrushes, and more. A heron rookery is located at the northern end of the park.

Long ago the Mercer Slough area was part of the vast marshlands that surrounded Lake Washington. Native peoples lived here, hunting muskrat and small mammals, fishing for salmon, and gathering edible roots and berries. In 1916, when the Ship Canal project lowered Lake Washington by 9 feet, the area could no longer support people whose livelihood depended on the bounty of the marshlands.

Today, 6 miles of trails, both paved and wood-chipped, twist through and around these preserved 320 acres. Overlake Blueberry Farm (open in season) and the historic Winters House add variety to a walk along Mercer Slough.

Footbridge over Mercer Slough's serene waters

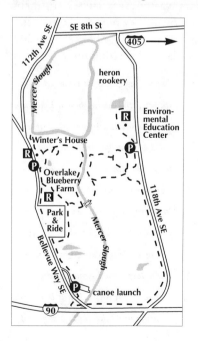

*How to Get There:* From I-90 just east of Mercer Island, east- or westbound, take exit 9 (Bellevue Way). Go about 0.25 mile north on Bellevue Way and park at the canoe launch, Park and Ride, or at Winter's House. Limited parking also along 118th Ave SE. Bellevue Parks (206) 455-6881. Mercer Slough Office (206) 462-2752.

# #52
# ROBINSWOOD PARK

BELLEVUE, 4 MILES SOUTHEAST OF DOWNTOWN

| | |
|---|---|
| HIGHLIGHTS | *Forest, pond, lawns, bird-watching* |
| TRAIL | *1 mile total; paved, gravel, and natural surfaces* |
| OTHER USAGE | *Bicycles on paved trails* |
| STEEPNESS | *Level to gentle* |
| CONNECTING TRAILS | *Lake-to-Lake Trail (via streets)* |
| PARK SERVICES | *Restrooms, picnic shelter, playground, tennis center, hospitality/retreat center* |
| DISABLED ACCESS | *Restrooms, picnic areas, playground, buildings* |

AS THOUGH THEY KNOW THE PARK IS NAMED FOR THEM, THE RED-breasted robins whinny, and call *tut tut tut* as they hop slowly from the needle-lined path to the salal bushes. This rectangle of green, neighborhood park so close to I-90 provides lawns for lazing on, a pond to explore, and a mile of trails through open forest.

If you sometimes feel closed in by the dense Northwest forest, this is a good park to explore, with its more open glades. Begin near Robinswood House on 148th Avenue SE and, if there are no wedding guests milling about, explore the secluded garden behind the house. Then head into the forest of Douglas fir and madrona.

The trail makes weblike loops, leading finally to steps and the paved Lake-to-Lake Trail along the southern boundary. Turn east toward 156th Avenue SE and re-

**Forest Playgrounds?** *Downed logs, stumps, and spring board holes are not gymnastic equipment. These dead trees might look big and tough, but they're not. Scrambling feet and grabbing hands break off the moss and bark, which harbor the insects that birds eat. Many young saplings can grow only on nurse logs. Teach your children to respect what has taken a long time to grow but takes only a moment to kill.*

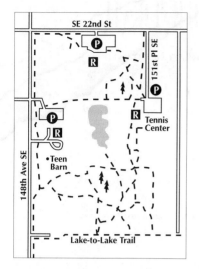

enter the forest heading north, where it seems light, even on overcast days. As is characteristic of young Douglas firs, the lower branches have fallen off as the upper ones seek light. The result: a forest of poles under an umbrella of green. The undergrowth of salal and Oregon grape is clearly visible, as are the robins and wrens who perch in the low shrubs. On this gently padded natural trail, your feet make no sound, so the birds are less quick to fly.

Soon you emerge at a green, manicured lawn, where a small pond attracts kids with model boats and ducks seeking food. In spring you'll likely see a female mallard with her brood of peeping ducklings. To the east is the tennis center, but heading north returns you to forest and more quiet walking before you emerge at the playing fields.

*How to Get There:* From I-90 east of Lake Washington, eastbound, take exit 11B (148th Ave SE) and head north. The park is on the right just after SE 28th St.

From I-90 east of Mercer Island, westbound, take exit 11 (161st Ave SE, 156th Ave SE, 150th Ave SE). Follow signs to 148th Ave SE and proceed as above. Bellevue Parks (206) 455-6881.

# #53
# SPIRITRIDGE TRAIL

**BELLEVUE, 5.5 MILES SOUTHEAST OF DOWNTOWN**

| | |
|---|---|
| HIGHLIGHTS | *Quiet greenbelt, ponds* |
| TRAIL | *1.4 miles one way; gravel and natural surfaces* |
| OTHER USAGE | *Bicycles* |
| STEEPNESS | *Level to moderate* |
| CONNECTING TRAILS | *Robinswood Park (Walk #52) via Lake-to-Lake Trail* |
| PARK SERVICES | *Playground, picnic area, tennis, basketball* |
| DISABLED ACCESS | *Spiritridge Park only* |

TUCKED BETWEEN THE CONCRETE BUTTRESSES OF BOEING COMPUTER Services and a quiet suburban neighborhood, this walk provides just the right mix of greenery, soft trail, and easy access. Created by Boeing in

**Bell-shaped flowers brighten the glossy green foliage of native salal bushes**

1990 to buffer nearby homes from its parking lots and buildings, this semi-circular strip of land 1.4 miles long has been developed into a neighborhood sanctuary and a Bellevue city park.

A few old snags stand proud among the young madronas and cedars, inviting downy and hairy woodpeckers to tap for a meal. Small ponds provide habitat for ducks and frogs, and the undergrowth is lush with native thimbleberry, salal, and Oregon grape. Slowly, root by root, the city is aiming to rid this greenbelt of nonnative intrusive plants like the Himalayan blackberry and English ivy.

This is a gentle trail, one to keep in mind for a quick stop off I-90, a playground break for restless kids, or a short extention from Robinswood Park (Walk #52).

**How to Get There:** From I-90 in Bellevue, eastbound, take exit 11A (150th Ave SE, 156th Ave SE). Go over the freeway and turn right on Eastgate Way. Continue through the light at 156th Ave SE and turn left on 161st Ave SE. Spiritridge Park is on the right in 0.2 mile. The trail is on the left.

From I-90 in Bellevue, westbound, take exit 11 (161st Ave SE). Head north on 161st Ave SE for less than 0.2 mile to the park. Bellevue Parks (206) 455-6881.

# #54
# COAL CREEK PARK

BELLEVUE, 5.5 MILES SOUTH OF DOWNTOWN

| | |
|---|---|
| HIGHLIGHTS | *Forest, streams, historical site* |
| TRAIL | *4.3 miles total; natural surface* |
| OTHER USAGE | *Pedestrians only; no bicycles* |
| STEEPNESS | *Gentle to moderate* |
| CONNECTING TRAILS | *Cougar Mountain Regional Wildland Park (Walk #55)* |
| PARK SERVICES | *None* |
| DISABLED ACCESS | *None* |

LIKE A GREEN FINGER BECKONING FROM THE SUMMIT OF COUGAR Mountain toward Lake Washington, Coal Creek Park entices those looking for a low-elevation wildlands walk. Leave your car and let the forest surround you with tangled masses of ferns, blackberries, maples, and cedars. From the western (lower) end, the trail closely parallels Coal Creek. Old fallen trees lie across the sand-and-dirt trail, their mossy coats worn away by countless feet passing over them. In some, notches scar the trunks where volunteers have cut steps for fellow hikers.

Coal Creek Trail climbs steadily for 3 miles to the Red Town Trailhead of Cougar Mountain Regional Wildland Park (Walk #55). Although there are a few tangent trails leading up to housing developments on the ridge or to streamside viewpoints, the main trail is fairly clear and often marked with bright plastic tags.

Carved wooden signposts give directions and trail mileages. To make a loop of the walk, follow the Primrose Trail off to the left, which will pass Sandstone Falls 1.4 miles from the trailhead. Further along you pass a side trail to Skazo mine. This, like other abandoned mines, must be viewed from afar; signs at the Cougar Mountain trailhead just above here warn of odorless, colorless gases that may be present in any mine shaft. The Primrose Trail continues up a steep hillside, then joins the relatively larger, better-maintained Coal Creek Trail. Turn right to complete the loop, or left to meet up with other Cougar Mountain trails at Red Town Trailhead.

Not a trail for the timid, this one challenges with narrow ridges, a few steep, slippery stretches and, after a good rain, the possibility of a washout. If you're equal to it, all of this adds up to the pleasure of a few hours spent in sylvan wildness.

*How to Get There:* **From I-405 south of downtown Bellevue, north- or south-bound, take exit 10 (Coal Creek Pkwy, Factoria). Turn east (right if northbound, left if southbound) onto Coal Creek Pkwy SE. Go about 1.25 miles (past the light at Forest Drive SE). At the low point of the dip in the road, look on the left for a gravel parking lot where the trail begins. King County Parks (206) 296-4232.**

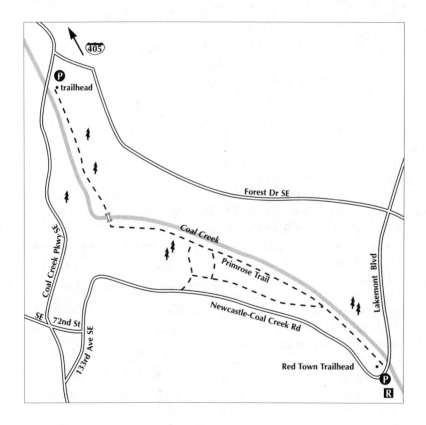

# #55
# COUGAR MOUNTAIN REGIONAL WILDLAND PARK
## (RED TOWN TRAILHEAD)

### NEAR BELLEVUE, 8.5 MILES SOUTHEAST OF DOWNTOWN

| | |
|---|---|
| HIGHLIGHTS | *Forest, historical sites* |
| TRAIL | *1 mile to 47 miles; gravel and natural surfaces* |
| OTHER USAGE | *Horses on some trails; no bicycles allowed* |
| STEEPNESS | *Gentle to steep* |
| CONNECTING TRAILS | *Coal Creek Park (Walk #54)* |
| PARK SERVICES | *Restrooms, maps, guided walks in summer* |
| DISABLED ACCESS | *None* |

THE WILD COUGAR MOUNTAIN PARK IS EVEN MORE INVITING NOW THAT it's being groomed but not tamed. In its forest you'll find wildlife, streams, cliffs, ravines, and history. Deer, bobcat, porcupine, and black bear roam the 3,000 acres, and many species of forest-dwelling songbirds live in the canopy or in the lush undergrowth. Here, too, you'll see evidence of long-ago logging and mining.

To understand, and come to love, Cougar Mountain, with its 47 miles of trails, you need to start one step at a time. You may have read about its labyrinth of trails that could foil a maze-trained lab-oratory rat, and given up in despair. Now, thanks to massive efforts by King County Parks and the Issaquah Alps Trails Club (all volunteers), Cougar is becoming a walker-friendly place. And the Red Town Trailhead is the best place from which to take an introductory walk.

**When You Run Out of Breadcrumbs:**

*No map? Explore a park the way you do a maze: by "keeping one hand on the wall." Continue taking right turns. This could take a while in Bridle Trails Park or on Cougar Mountain. Best to develop a good sense of direction.*

At the parking lot, take a map from the information board. Notice that south is at the top. Many loop walks are possible, ranging in length from half a mile to many miles. Start small, and increase your distances as you become familiar with the trail markings and the map.

For a good introduction, try W1, the Wildside Trail. Angling due south from the parking lot, it passes a sign warning of danger from gases (mainly $CO_2$) in mines. Believe it, heed it, but don't panic. You will be on well-traveled, open-air trails, not crawling through mine shafts. Wildside is a natural trail that crosses bridges and threads through a vegetation restoration project, an example of the dedicated care of the Trails Club volunteers. Make a loop back onto W2, Red Town Trail for a sampler. On your next visit, branch out. Have fun.

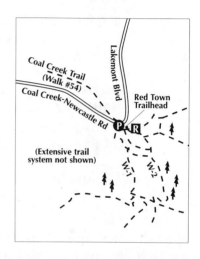

*How to Get There:* From I-90 in Bellevue, east- or westbound, take exit 13 (Newport Way, W Lake Sammamish Pkwy). Eastbound, turn right at the end of the ramp, then right again onto Newport Way. Westbound, turn left at the end of the ramp, go under the freeway, then turn right on Newport Way. Go 1 mile and turn left (south) on 164th Ave SE. Go 1.3 miles to Lakemont Blvd and turn right. Continue about 1.5 miles to the trailhead on the left.

From I-405 south of downtown Bellevue, north- or southbound, take exit 10 (Coal Creek Pkwy, Factoria). Turn east (right if northbound, left if southbound) onto Coal Creek Pkwy SE. Go about 2.5 miles to the shopping center. Turn left on SE 72nd St, then left again on Newcastle–Coal Creek Road. In about 2 miles look for the trailhead on the right. Summer guided walks (206) 296-4171. King County Parks (206) 296-4232. Issaquah Alps Trails Club (206) 328-0480.

# #56
# LUTHER BURBANK PARK

### MERCER ISLAND, 6 MILES SOUTHWEST OF BELLEVUE, 6 MILES SOUTHEAST OF SEATTLE

| | |
|---|---|
| HIGHLIGHTS | *Lakeshore, off-leash area, historical site, wetlands, art* |
| TRAIL | *1.5 miles total; paved and natural surfaces* |
| OTHER USAGE | *Bicycles* |
| STEEPNESS | *Level to gentle; some steps to lake* |
| CONNECTING TRAILS | *None* |
| PARK SERVICES | *Restrooms, tennis courts, playground, swimming beach, boat docks* |
| DISABLED ACCESS | *Picnic areas, restrooms, paved trails* |

YOU CAN ALMOST IMAGINE THE VAST HAND OF THE LAKE WASHINGTON spirit reaching over this northeastern corner of Mercer Island, holding back the surrounding suburbia to preserve this stretch of land. With its grassy meadows and neatly tended lawns, pockets of berries and bogs, Luther Burbank Park offers breathing space and expansive views across the lake to Bellevue and Seattle.

Once the grounds of a home for wayward Seattle boys, these 77 acres retain a few reminders of days past. Two sturdy brick buildings, one now housing the administration offices for King County Parks, are all that remain intact of the Boys Parental Home (later Luther Burbank School). When you walk north from the building past the elegant poplar and cottonwood trees, stop and explore the ruins of the old barn. For over 50 years, Holstein cows grazed where boat-watchers sit today on the gentle hills of Luther Burbank.

At Calkins Point on the northern tip, a marshland harbors frogs and ducks as well as red-winged blackbirds. Bear right and walk south along the waterfront, past the buildings to the docks, tennis courts, and picnic areas. If you've come with kids, plan on a long pause at the playground. This one was created by someone with a fertile imagination: brick hills

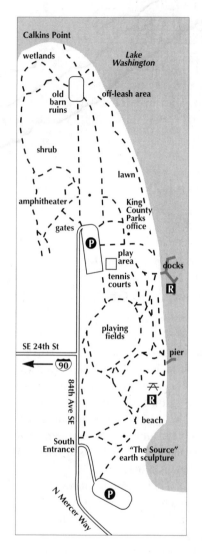

to climb, endless slides, and swings—all cushioned with tire chips for safe landings.

When you can lure the kids off the brick mountains, head south across the meadow to explore the earth sculpture with its furrows and hills. What a great landscape for make-believe forts or wild games of tag. In summer, the grassy bumps and the nearby beach ring out with the calls of children. Complete the loop with a stroll north again along the water's edge, past secret hideouts for the lake's feathered inhabitants, ending at the docks.

*How to Get There:* From I-90 on Mercer Island, eastbound, take exit 7A (77th Ave SE). Turn left at the stop sign, go across the freeway, then turn right. Continue straight at the stop light near the Park and Ride and turn left onto 81st Ave SE. Go to the stop and turn right on SE 24th St. When the road curves right, go left into the park.

From I-90 on Mercer Island, westbound, take exit 7 (Island Crest Way). At the top of the ramp veer right following signs. Turn left on 84th Ave SE to enter the park. King County Parks (206) 296-4232.

# #57
# PIONEER PARK
## (MERCER ISLAND)

CENTRAL MERCER ISLAND, 7 MILES SOUTHWEST OF BELLEVUE,
7 MILES EAST OF SEATTLE

| | |
|---|---|
| HIGHLIGHTS | *Forest* |
| TRAIL | *5 miles total; paved and natural surfaces* |
| OTHER USAGE | *Pedestrians only; horses allowed in NW section* |
| STEEPNESS | *Gentle to moderate* |
| CONNECTING TRAILS | *None* |
| PARK SERVICES | *None; guide book for sale at Mercer Island Parks office, $1* |
| DISABLED ACCESS | *Paved sidewalk along Island Crest Way* |

WANDER A LABYRINTH OF TRAILS THROUGH SOUND-BLANKETING FOREST in this touch of wildness in the center of Mercer Island. Raccoons leave footprints on the dirt trails and squirrels chatter from the branches.

Logged about 70 years ago, the forest now supports a variety of second-growth trees, including alder, maple, madrona, western hemlock, and Douglas fir. Many have English ivy (an unwanted volunteer from nearby homes) clinging to their trunks like shaggy blankets or display a fine coating of blue-green lichen on their northern sides.

Park on Island Crest Way and dive in. Trails meander through each of the three sections of the park. You can choose the company of horses (in the northwest section only) or not, and choose level (northeast section) or sloping (southeast section) land. With many kid-created side trails, you could possibly get lost, or at least end up in someone's backyard. To maintain your bearings, listen for the traffic on Island Crest Way, and in the southeast section remember that uphill leads to the west and Island Crest.

Try a winter walk here, when the cold has hardened the dirt trails. With the leaves gone, you can look out through the sinewy forms of naked branches to the lake. Oregon grape, sword ferns, cedars, and hemlock all shimmer in vibrant green against the browns and grays of winter bark.

*How to Get There:* From I-90 on Mercer Island, eastbound, take exit 7B (Island Crest Way). The ramp leads directly onto Island Crest Way. Go about 3.2 miles and park at the corner of SE 68th St and Island Crest Way.

From I-90 on Mercer Island, westbound, take exit 7 (Island Crest Way). Turn left at the top of the ramp and cross the freeway. Go straight on Island Crest Way, about 3.3 miles and park at the corner of SE 68th St and Island Crest Way. The three sections of the park intersect here. Mercer Island Parks (206) 236-3545.

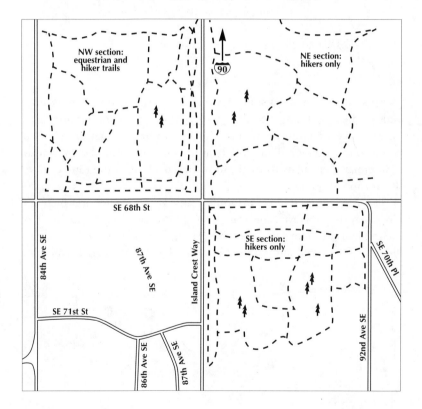

# #58

# BEAVER LAKE PARK

### SAMMAMISH PLATEAU, 15 MILES EAST OF BELLEVUE

HIGHLIGHTS *Lake, forest, stream, art, wetlands*

TRAIL *1-mile loop; natural surface*

OTHER USAGE *Pedestrians only*

STEEPNESS *Level to gentle*

CONNECTING TRAILS *None*

PARK SERVICES *Restrooms, picnic shelter, fishing area, playground, playing fields, conference lodge, brochure*

DISABLED ACCESS *Restrooms, picnic shelter*

IN THIS SANCTUARY FROM SUBURBIA ON THE PLATEAU, SILENCE IS BROKEN only by the call of birds and the trickle of the creek. Four-hundred-acre Beaver Lake is an interesting mix of amenities, art, and nature. The two totem poles, Salmon Pole and Beaver Pole, are examples of British Columbian Tsimshian art by David Boxley, paid for by the King County 1% for the Arts Fund.

The 1-mile loop trail begins south of the picnic shelter, in which are displayed three Native American house posts from Upper Skagit tribes carved by David Horsley—again, with King County arts funds. Pass the Beaver Totem Pole and enter the forest. The trail loosely follows the

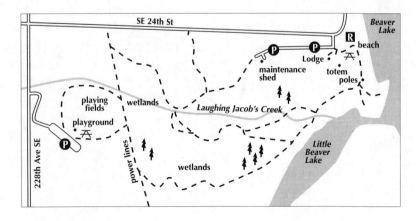

lake edge and then turns west to cross Laughing Jacob's Creek. Huge snags tell of giant trees felled by wind or fire.

Several narrow trails branch off, but stick to the widest path until it emerges under the power lines. Ahead lie the playing fields and playground. You can retrace your steps from here or take a right under the power lines, then a right again where the trail begins to climb a knoll. Look for a clear path entering the forest; again, follow the widest trail to emerge behind the park maintenance shed, near the main parking lot.

In recent years, toads were the memorable wildlife attraction of the park, at least during a few weeks twice a year. Each spring, in April or May, hundreds of adult Western toads migrated en masse back to their breeding grounds at Beaver Lake. By midsummer, the metamorphosed young toadlets journeyed through the park and across the road to drier forest where they matured.

British Columbian Tsimshian totem poles greet visitors to Beaver Lake Park

*How to Get There:* From I-90 east of Bellevue, east- or westbound, take exit 17 (Front St, E Lake Sammamish Pkwy). Turn north (left if eastbound, right if westbound) on Front St (which becomes E Lake Sammamish Pkwy). Go 2 miles and turn right on SE 43rd St (which becomes 228th Ave SE). Go 2.5 miles and turn right on SE 24th St. The park is on the right in 1.5 miles.

From I-405 in Bellevue, north- or southbound, take exit 14 (SR 520, Redmond) east to Redmond. Exit onto Hwy 202 (Redmond–Fall City Rd). Go 2.5 miles and turn right on Sahalee Way NE (which becomes 228th Ave SE). Go 5.4 miles and turn left on SE 24th St. Continue 1.5 miles to the park, on the right. King County Parks (206) 296-4232.

# #59
# TOLT RIVER–
# JOHN MACDONALD PARK

CARNATION, 19 MILES EAST OF BELLEVUE

| | |
|---|---|
| HIGHLIGHTS | *River, forest, Cascade views, bird-watching* |
| TRAIL | *3 miles total; natural surface* |
| OTHER USAGE | *Bicycles* |
| STEEPNESS | *Gentle to steep* |
| CONNECTING TRAILS | *None* |
| PARK SERVICES | *Restrooms, picnic shelters, playing fields, seasonal campgrounds* |
| DISABLED ACCESS | *Restrooms, suspension bridge, some campsites, picnic areas* |

NESTLED IN THE SNOQUALMIE VALLEY FARMLANDS, THIS PARK AT THE confluence of the Tolt and Snoqualmie Rivers boasts lovely riverside and forested-hill walking. A graceful, 500-foot suspension bridge spans the Snoqualmie, linking the fields on the east to the wooded hills on the west.

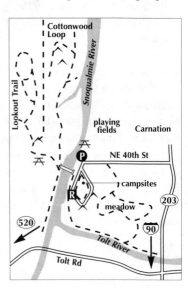

If you're lucky, you may see white-tailed deer, black-tailed deer or, less likely, coyotes wandering the forest and riverbanks. Keep your eye out for hawks, osprey, and eagles wheeling overhead or perched on snags above the river.

Several random miles of trails criss-cross the western hills. Flat, sandy trails lead both north and south from the bridge, with covered picnic shelters available all year. The trail directly uphill west of the bridge passes campsites that

The suspension bridge that spans the Snoqualmie River offers valley and mountain views

are available from April through October.

To gain some elevation, take the trail north from the bridge and, after about a mile, angle left onto Cottonwood Loop. Follow the contour of the hill, turning uphill onto Lookout Trail. There, you'll find yourself in the treetops, from which you can look down on the meadows and across to Mount Si and the nearby Cascades. On clear days, the suspension bridge offers all the elevation you need to see the rocky summer contours or the early-winter dusting of snow on Three Fingers Mountain to the north (downstream) and Tiger Mountain and the Issaquah Alps (upstream).

A hundred years ago, the confluence of the Tolt and Snoqualmie Rivers was the site of the largest of the four main villages of the Snoqualmie Tribe. Home to possibly more than a thousand people in 18 longhouses, the village was considered the capital of this rich tribe, which formed trading relations with tribes from eastern Washington across Snoqualmie Pass.

*How to Get There:* From I-405 in Bellevue, north- or southbound, take exit 14 (SR 520, Redmond) east. Follow it to the end in Redmond and take the Redmond–Fall City Rd exit. Go east about 7.8 miles and turn left on Tolt Hill Rd. Go 3.5 miles across the Snoqualmie River and turn left on Fall City–Carnation Rd (Hwy 203), crossing the Tolt river. Go 0.5 mile and turn left on NE 40th St into the park.

From I-90 east of Bellevue, eastbound, take exit 22 (Preston, Fall City). Head north on Hwy 203 about 9.5 miles through Fall City to Carnation. After crossing the Tolt River, turn left on NE 40th St into the park. King County Parks (206) 296-4232.

# #60
# TIGER MOUNTAIN
## (TRADITION LAKE PLATEAU)

### 14 MILES SOUTHEAST OF BELLEVUE

| | |
|---|---|
| HIGHLIGHTS | *Forest, lakes, wetlands* |
| TRAIL | *1 to many miles; gravel and natural surfaces* |
| OTHER USAGE | *Horses and bicycles allowed on designated trails* |
| STEEPNESS | *Gentle; some trails moderate to steep* |
| CONNECTING TRAILS | *Many trails on Tiger Mountain* |
| PARK SERVICES | *Restrooms, picnic shelters* |
| DISABLED ACCESS | *Restrooms, Around the Lake trail* |

TO CHOOSE ONE WALK ON TIGER MOUNTAIN IS LIKE BEING LED TO A smorgasbord and then told to taste only one dish. Tiger Mountain, like its neighbor Cougar Mountain, must be sampled on many repeat trips. Both areas, because they are wildlands, challenge the timid walker with their numerous side trails and their sometimes-unmarked intersections. Start with one well-trodden, well-signposted trail. Learn the trailhead area, become familiar with the names of other trails, and then add them, one by one, to your hiking menu.

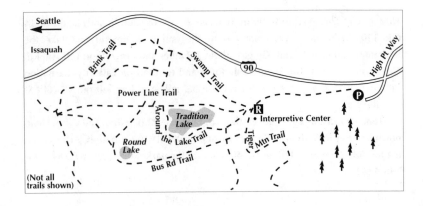

Tradition Lake Plateau is only a few minutes from Issaquah and has 13 trails to choose from. Many are level or nearly level. Most are signed. From the parking area, pass through the gate and follow the road as it gradually climbs to the power lines. Turn left to find the restrooms, interpretive signs, and map. If you don't have a map in hand (see below), choose

**Rustic bridges and well-developed trails crisscross Tradition Lake Plateau**

either the Around the Lake Trail or the Bus Trail for starters; both are clearly signed. The Around the Lake Trail is newly graded for wheelchair accessibility. Follow its level wanderings on a hillside in lush forest. Down to your right, you'll see glimpses of Tradition Lake—in winter a full body of water, in summer half mint fields and marsh and half water. There are no trails close to the water's edge in order to protect the fragile habitat of the many woodland animals who live there, but the distance only adds to the lake's charm: a tantalizing glimpse of gentle reflections on pristine water.

After the second interpretive sign along the trail, wheelchairs need to turn back. At this point the crunching gravel gives way to a soft trail, crossed by many roots. In spring, wildflowers such as western trillium and vanilla leaf brighten the shadows under the Douglas fir and western red cedar. Pale green new growth on the lady ferns uncurls like sleeping caterpillars. Continue on around Tradition Lake, returning via the Power Line Trail, or take a small trail to the left and emerge on the wide, smooth Bus Trail. Right takes you deeper onto the plateau trails, and to Round Lake; left returns you, past the old Scenicruiser bus wreck, to the trailhead.

*How to Get There:* **From I-90 east of Bellevue, eastbound, take exit 20 (High Point Way). At the end of the exit ramp turn right and then right again onto the frontage road. Park along the side. Maps are available at the Chamber of Commerce in Issaquah for $2.50. Department of Natural Resources (360) 825-1631, Issaquah Alps Trails Club (206) 328-0480.**

# #61
# PRESTON–
# SNOQUALMIE FALLS TRAIL

**PRESTON, EAST OF ISSAQUAH, 17 MILES SOUTHEAST OF BELLEVUE**

| | |
|---|---|
| HIGHLIGHTS | *Forest, Snoqualmie Falls view* |
| TRAIL | *6 miles one way; paved, with one short, unpaved stretch* |
| OTHER USAGE | *Bicycles* |
| STEEPNESS | *Level to steep* |
| CONNECTING TRAILS | *None* |
| PARK SERVICES | *Restrooms* |
| DISABLED ACCESS | *Whole trail except area with switchbacks (to reach viewpoint, begin at Alice Lake Road)* |

JUST MINUTES EAST OF ISSAQUAH, THE TINY TOWN OF PRESTON, KNOWN mainly for its past days of logging glory, now hosts the trailhead of one of the region's loveliest paved rails-to-trails walkways. Those who walk the trail to the end are rewarded with a stunning, long-distance view of Snoqualmie Falls.

From the Preston trailhead, walk east through a quiet forest of maple, red alder, and Douglas fir. The trail stays high on a ridge above the road and the Raging River, but little traffic noise comes through the foliage. Footbridges cross small streams where you can imagine the raccoons and possums coming for early-morning drinks. Just before crossing the Preston–Fall City Road, at about 2 miles, the trail makes a sharp switchback and drops steeply. Be cautious when you cross here; there is no crosswalk, and cars are moving fast. On the far side, follow the off-road path back to the west for 1,000 feet until it turns left into a small neigh-

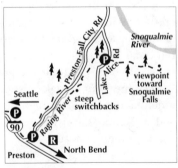

Relax at trail's end for an uncommon view of Snoqualmie Falls

borhood. Here it crosses the Raging River. Ahead is a short climb, with switchbacks and a few steps. Take this to rejoin the paved trail.

Back in the forest, the trail now runs high above the road, again exchanging the traffic sounds to those of birds. A high trestle bridge takes you over a forested gorge. From the Alice Lake Road and parking lot, the trail continues another level 1.9 miles. Here, at the easternmost end, you can rest on a bench while looking through a forest-framed view to the white beauty of Snoqualmie Falls.

*How to Get There:* From I-90 east of Bellevue, eastbound, take exit 22 (Preston, Fall City). Go left over the freeway then right onto Preston–Fall City Rd (to the left is SE High Point Way). Pass the Preston store and look for the marked trailhead.

To begin at Alice Lake Rd go about 3.4 miles on Preston–Fall City Rd to SE 47th St. Turn right, then right again on Lake Alice Rd. Go about 1.5 miles to the parking lot and trail crossing. There is no trailhead in Fall City. King County Parks (206) 296-4232.

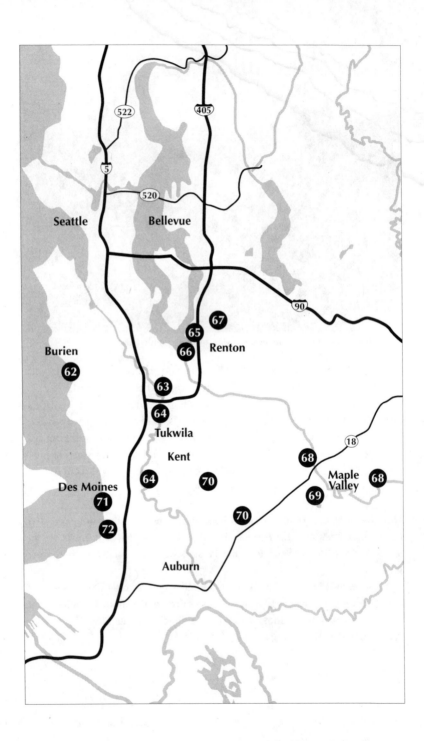

# IN AND AROUND DES MOINES, RENTON, AND KENT

# #62
# SEAHURST (ED MUNRO) PARK

BURIEN, ON PUGET SOUND, 11 MILES SOUTH OF SEATTLE

HIGHLIGHTS *Saltwater beach, Olympic views, forest*
TRAIL *2 miles; paved and natural surfaces*
OTHER USAGE *Pedestrians only*
STEEPNESS *Level or steep*
CONNECTING TRAILS *None*
PARK SERVICES *Restrooms, picnic shelters, playground, Marine Technology Lab (open to the public)*
DISABLED ACCESS *Restrooms, paved trail, picnic areas*

A RUGGED RAVINE AND A MATURE FOREST OF BIGLEAF MAPLES AND conifers welcome you to this park-by-the-Sound. Unmapped trails lace the steep, fern-strewn hillsides under moss-draped trees. The beach, at high or low tide, feels wild and open. Views extend west to Vashon Island and the Olympics. Bald eagles may soar above the water, where loons and grebes dive for fish.

Just minutes west of Sea-Tac Airport, this park is a microcosm of Puget Sound forest and tidal habitat. At low tide, the gently sloping beach invites exploration. Although the Seahurst beach has no rock-lined tide pools, small puddles preserve gallons of the last high tide, and in them often lounge colorful kelp crabs and red rock crabs. Also common are the smaller beach crabs, about 1.5 inches across the body—the

**A misted spider web glistens in a flash of afternoon sunlight**

greenish hairy beach crab and its purplish companion.

If the tide is high, or if you prefer dry feet, you can stroll the path above the sea wall for almost a mile each way. The steep forest trails are not well maintained and are obstructed with blow-downs, but according to park rangers, it's a challenge to get lost: all trails lead to the park boundaries, to the parking lot, or back down to the beach.

*How to Get There:* **From I-5 just south of Seattle, northbound, take exit 154 (SR 518 west, Burien). Go west on SR 518 until it ends in Burien. Cross 1st Ave S onto 148th St. Turn right on Ambaum Blvd SW, go a few blocks and turn left onto SW 144th St (marked by a park sign). Go 3 blocks and turn right on 13th Ave SW (another park sign), which becomes SW 140th St as it winds down to the park.**

**From I-5 just south of Seattle, southbound, take exit 154B (SR 518, Burien, Sea-Tac Airport) onto SR 518 heading west to Burien. Proceed as above. King County Parks (206) 296-4281.**

*Caught in the Web: Late-summer and fall walks on little-used trails mean "web-in-the-face hiking." Two options: wave a (dead) fern frond in the air in front of you as you hike, or generously offer to take place number two in line. Feign innocence when your companion turns round to glare at you with a spider on her nose. The upside to webs: damp with mist or morning dew, they glisten like silver necklaces on the branches. Undoubtedly one of nature's finer works of art.*

# #63
# FORT DENT PARK

### Tukwila, 13 miles southeast of Seattle

| | |
|---|---|
| HIGHLIGHTS | *Pond, river, art* |
| TRAIL | *1 mile around open spaces and perimeter; paved and natural surfaces* |
| OTHER USAGE | *Bicycles* |
| STEEPNESS | *Level* |
| CONNECTING TRAILS | *Duwamish/Green River Trail (Walk #64)* |
| PARK SERVICES | *Restrooms, picnic tables, playing fields* |
| DISABLED ACCESS | *Restrooms, section of Duwamish/Green River Trail (Walk #64)* |

THIS LARGE, GRASSY PARK OFFERS A POND, OPEN PLAYING FIELDS, AND casual walking on the perimeter trail. Located just at the I-405 interchange near Southcenter, Fort Dent Park has a surprisingly green, rural feel. And the Canada geese, mallards, and other waterfowl that frequent the pond seem content to visit a park, not a wilderness.

But wilderness it was, a century and a half ago when the U.S. Infantry posted a regiment here to protect the pioneer settlers in the Duwamish, Black, and Green River Valleys. Back then, Fort Dent served not only as an outpost but as a river landing for the passenger- and goods-carrying vessels on the river. (That's the Black River, one of those now-mythical waterways that virtually dried up after 1916 with the building of the Lake Washington Ship Canal.)

Today, the only reminder of Fort Dent is a monument placed

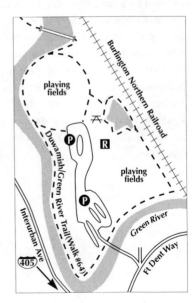

by the Tukwila Historical Society about 250 yards south of the site of the original 1856 stockade. What a shock those infantrymen would have now, coming back to find not one remnant of either the fort or the river.

If you're in the area and want a quick leg stretch, or if you're here to see a cricket or soccer game, this makes a satisfying walk in open air through a landscaped park. It's also a great starting point for the Duwamish/Green River Trail (Walk #64).

*How to Get There:* From I-5 south of Seattle, northbound, take exit 154 (I-405 north to Renton). From I-405 take exit 1 (SR 181, Tukwila, W Valley Hwy). Turn left off the exit ramp and go under the freeway. Just after crossing the river turn right on Ft Dent Way into a business park. At the traffic divider turn left over small bridge into the park.

From I-5 south of Seattle, southbound, take exit 154B (Southcenter Blvd). At the end of the ramp go under the freeway and turn right on Southcenter Blvd. Go about 1 mile (through several lights) and turn left on Interurban Ave S. Cross the river and proceed as above.

From I-405 south of Bellevue, southbound, take exit 1 (SR 181 south, Tukwila, W Valley Hwy). Turn right (north) on Interurban Ave S. Take an immediate right on Ft Dent Way and proceed as above. King County Parks (206) 296-4281.

Stately Canada geese glide the pond at Fort Dent Park

# #64
# DUWAMISH/GREEN RIVER TRAIL

**TUKWILA (13 MILES SOUTHEAST OF SEATTLE) TO KENT
(20 MILES NORTHEAST OF TACOMA)**

|  |  |
|---|---|
| HIGHLIGHTS | *River, Cascade and Mount Rainier views, bird-watching* |
| TRAIL | *8 miles one way (with breaks and unconnected sections); paved* |
| OTHER USAGE | *Bicycles* |
| STEEPNESS | *Level* |
| CONNECTING TRAILS | *Fort Dent Park (Walk #63), via roads: Interurban Trail (via streets)* |
| PARK SERVICES | *Restrooms, picnic shelters, playgrounds, boat launch at Briscoe Park* |
| DISABLED ACCESS | *Restrooms, trail at Fort Dent Park (Walk #63), Bicentennial Park, and Briscoe Park* |

A SLICE OF PEACE BETWEEN LIGHT INDUSTRY, SHOPPING MALLS, AND freeways, the Duwamish/Green River Trail teases with reminders of a less-industrialized time in the Tukwila/Kent region. Red-winged blackbirds still nest in the reeds, and migrant waterfowl make bright patches of color on the river under winter skies. Though you're never free of the noise of civilization, the river flows gently along beside the trail, and views of the Cascades and Mount Rainier lift the spirits.

Mile by mile, this paved riverside walkway has become a reality, with more improvement to come. For now, the best starting point is either Bicentennial Park in Tukwila or Briscoe Park in Kent.

From Bicentennial Park you can walk half a mile north along the river to I-405 and then, if the pathway is passable (it was under construction in 1996), follow it north, across Interurban Avenue and into Fort Dent Park(Walk #63). For the next mile you skirt the landscaped edge of Fort Dent Park and cross the footbridge that marks the junction of the (now mainly dry) Black River and the Green River.

Heading south from Bicentennial, the trail hugs the riverbank. Wayside parks offer restrooms and playgrounds, as well as tiny rectangular green spaces along the way. Where the river makes a sharp U

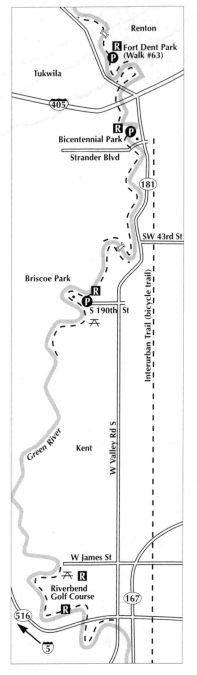

curve, a lovely footbridge spans it, now offering walks on either side. (If you don't cross, the trail soon peters out into industry.) On the south side, a left turn will take you to a street and a trailhead; a right turn takes you south into Kent and, in about a mile or so, to Briscoe Park. Here you'll find park amenities including disabled access, parking, and a boat launch. Follow the trail south another mile until it reaches streets.

Farther south, another peaceful stretch along the Green River can be found at Kent's Riverbend Golf Course. Stroll the perimeter of the course along the river, making a 3-mile trip to Washington Street (SR 181) and back.

***How to Get There:*** To begin in Fort Dent Park: see directions for Walk #63.

To begin at Bicentennial Park: From I-405 in Tukwila north- or southbound, take exit 1 (SR 181 south, Tukwila, W Valley Hwy). Turn south (left from Interurban Ave S under the freeway if southbound, or right if northbound), on W Valley Hwy (SR 181). Go 0.4 mile and turn right on Strander Blvd. Cross the river and turn right into the park.

To begin at Briscoe Park: Continue south on W Valley Hwy and turn right on S 190th St. Follow 190th St to the end and go straight into the first parking lot. Take the stairs up to the trail. Tukwila Parks (206) 433-1858. Kent Parks (206) 859-3992.

# #65

# GENE COULON MEMORIAL BEACH PARK

RENTON, 8.5 MILES SOUTH OF BELLEVUE

| | |
|---|---|
| HIGHLIGHTS | *Lake, bird-watching, wetlands, views, art* |
| TRAIL | *1.5 miles one way; paved* |
| OTHER USAGE | *Pedestrians only* |
| STEEPNESS | *Level* |
| CONNECTING TRAILS | *None* |
| PARK SERVICES | *Restrooms, playground, two restaurants, boat launch, swimming beach, tennis courts, volleyball courts, picnic shelters, horseshoe pits, fishing pier* |
| DISABLED ACCESS | *Restrooms, buildings, trail* |

HUNDREDS OF COOTS, THEIR WHITE BILLS POKING THE GRASS FOR food, waddle awkwardly over the lawn. On the water, dozens of mallards, Canada geese, and gulls cavort and swim. Lining the log booms like sentries, the gulls declare their territory with raucous calls.

Gene Coulon is a long sliver of a park—in places, less than a hundred feet wide—sandwiched between Lake Washington and the Burlington Northern Railroad. Yet it's so carefully designed that its broad, level shore walk, landscaped with native plants and interpretive signs, attracts walkers year-round. In summer you share it with boisterous children and quiet sun-worshippers; in fall, winter, and spring you share it with waterfowl and fellow walkers.

Though the park is most heavily used in summer for its beach and boat launch, the lakeside walk has unexpected beauty in winter. Grasses are tawny yellow against the dark blue of the lake, and among the bare-stemmed bushes hang winter's boldest ornaments: white snowberries and red rose hips. As the trail traces the contours of the lake, it crosses marshes and miniature gardens of native plantings. Look for Trestle Marsh, where old pilings mark the former railroad, cedar mill, and log-

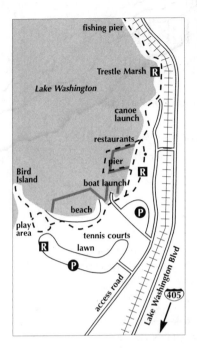

**But They're Such Fun to Feed!** *Most park authorities prohibit the feeding of waterfowl. Here's why:*

△ *Human food is junk food to waterfowl, with none of the nutrients they need. Undernourished birds are more susceptible to disease.*

△ *Feeding entices waterfowl to overwinter, which means more breeding pairs and an ever-increasing number of ducks and geese in our lakes. Waterfowl waste contains parasites that cause swimmer's itch, an allergic rash you wouldn't wish on anyone. Clean water means more swimming beaches.*

△ *Waterfowl waste not only pollutes, it also fertilizes aquatic weeds that choke out other plants and animals. You can't swim or fish in a choked lake.*

dumping site. In spring on Nature Island Bird Sanctuary you may see nesting mallards and Canada geese. In any season, you can add distance to your stroll by exploring the boardwalks that surround the floating picnic area.

*How to Get There:* **From I-5 in Renton, northbound, take exit 5 (SR 900, Issaquah, Sunset Blvd). Turn west (left) and go under the freeway on Park Ave. Cross the railroad tracks and take a hard right at the light onto Lake Washington Blvd N. The southern park entrance is on your left in a few hundred yards. Other parking is available if you continue on Lake Washington Blvd N.**

**From I-405 in Renton, southbound, take exit 5 (SR 900 east, Park Ave N, Sunset Blvd NE). Turn west (right) on Park Ave. Proceed as above. Renton Parks (206) 235-2568.**

# #66
# CEDAR RIVER TRAIL
## (NORTHWEST SECTION)

RENTON, 10.5 MILES SOUTH OF BELLEVUE

| | |
|---|---|
| HIGHLIGHTS | *River, manicured park, forest, art* |
| TRAIL | *4.75 miles one way; paved* |
| OTHER USAGE | *Bicycles* |
| STEEPNESS | *Level* |
| CONNECTING TRAILS | *None* |
| PARK SERVICES | *Restrooms, picnic shelters at parks* |
| DISABLED ACCESS | *Restrooms, picnic areas, trail in the city and at Cedar River Park and Riverview Park on the Maple Valley Highway* |

TO EXPERIENCE ONE OF THE BEST EXAMPLES OF URBAN GREENERY BY A river's edge, begin at the mouth of the Cedar River and walk south through a manicured park. After crossing under I-405 the trail changes to a more natural, forested setting.

The city end of this trail is well loved by families and office workers because of its easy access, park amenities, and proximity to the river. So close is the clear, shallow Cedar that when it rises only a foot at flood time, water covers the walkway. (Call the city after heavy rains.) At the library, which spans the river, continue south, past sculptures and through Liberty Park, with its swimming pool and playground. Street crossings take you under the I-405 trestle to the Community Center and another trailhead in Cedar River Park.

Access to this section begins with a pedestrian bridge across the Cedar River. From here the trail, still well paved, traverses fields and enters a cool second-growth forest. Visible through a veil of cottonwoods and alder, the Cedar River parallels the path. In summer, swallows swoop for insects over the water, and year-round, birds forage and sing in the maple and hemlock hillside to the south. Winding in and out of forest, and crossing the Cedar once again, the pavement continues to the golf course. Now gravel, it closely parallels the highway, more a bi-

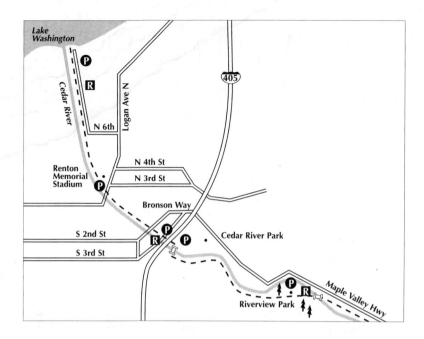

cycler's than a walker's trail. Pick it up again in Maple Valley for another wooded walk above the river. (See Walk #68, Cedar River Trail, southeast section.)

*How to Get There:* To begin at the northernmost end: From I-405 in Renton, northbound, take exit 4 (SR 169 south, Bronson Way, SR 900 west). Follow signs for 900 west. Turn right at the end of the ramp. Go under the freeway and cross Sunset Blvd N. Now on Bronson Way, cross the Cedar River and turn right (north) on Logan Ave S. Cross the river again and turn left on N 6th St, passing the Boeing buildings. Turn right at the gate and go 0.5 mile to parking.

From I-405 in Renton, southbound, take exit 5 (SR 900 east, Park Ave N, Sunset Blvd NE) and turn right on Park Dr. Pass the Boeing buildings, turn right on N 6th St, and proceed as above.

For the Community Center trailhead: From I-405 in Renton, northbound, take exit 4A (SR 169 south, Maple Valley Hwy) and go south on Maple Valley Hwy. Take the first right into Cedar River Park. From I-405 in Renton, southbound, take exit 4 and follow signs to SR 169 south (Enumclaw). At the second light, turn left on SR 169, go under the freeway, and take the first right into Cedar River Park. The trail is across the river behind the Community Center. Renton Parks (206) 235-2568.

# #67
# HONEY CREEK TRAIL

**RENTON, 10.5 MILES SOUTHEAST OF BELLEVUE**

|  |  |
|---|---|
| HIGHLIGHTS | *Stream, forested ravine* |
| TRAIL | *1 mile one way; gravel* |
| OTHER USAGE | *Bicycles* |
| STEEPNESS | *Level; moderate on NE 27th St* |
| CONNECTING TRAILS | *May Creek Trail* |
| PARK SERVICES | *None* |
| DISABLED ACCESS | *None* |

MAMMOTH, GNARLED MAPLES SUSPEND THEIR BRANCHES HIGH OVER the stream. Old fallen giants create natural bridges or serve as nurse logs for forest regeneration. This densely forested ravine along Honey

Ancient stumps nurture new life: huckleberry fern and hemlock

Creek shelters winter wrens, robins, shrews, moles, raccoons, coyotes, and more. Landslides have brought down trees and stumps, leaving a snapshot of the streambed's geological history.

Hidden below homes and apartments, this walk has long been a favorite for local residents. Now, thanks to a recent land acquisition by the City of Renton, the mile-long trail is entirely on public property. Trail access begins on the now-abandoned stretch of road called Devil's Elbow (an extension of NE 27th Street). At the utility station head upstream (south). The gravel utility trail soon decreases in width to allow a more intimate walk in this fine old ravine. Return when the gravel ends and the trail narrows to shoulder width in the undergrowth.

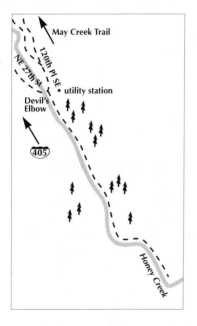

*How to Get There:* From I-405 in Renton, north- or southbound, take exit 6 (NE 30th St). Head east (right if northbound, left if southbound) on NE 30th St (which becomes Kennewick Pl N, then NE 27th St). Where NE 27th St veers sharply right you see a "road closed" sign straight ahead. Park along the curb and walk down the closed road, through the gates onto the abandoned Devil's Elbow. Honey Creek trail begins on the right (south side) behind the utility station. (The ravine to your left leads to May Creek Trail, accessed just east of the utility station on the opposite side of the road from Honey Creek Trail.) Renton Parks (206) 235-2568.

# #68
# CEDAR RIVER TRAIL
## (SOUTHEAST SECTION)

### Maple Valley, 20.5 miles southeast of Bellevue

| | |
|---|---|
| HIGHLIGHTS | *Forest, river, bird-watching* |
| TRAIL | *Over 6 miles one way; gravel rails-to-trails conversion* |
| OTHER USAGE | *Bicycles* |
| STEEPNESS | *Level* |
| CONNECTING TRAILS | *Lake Wilderness Trail* |
| PARK SERVICES | *None* |
| DISABLED ACCESS | *None* |

LINED WITH COTTONWOODS, ALDERS, AND MIXED CONIFERS, THIS converted rails-to-trails path is wide and smooth and offers year-round dry-footed walking. Fall is a particularly striking time to walk the Cedar River Trail, as colorful leaves echo the red, green and brown tones of the salmon returning to spawn. A wild cry might break the stillness as a

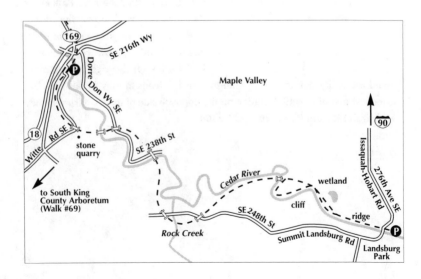

bald eagle rises from the river, a salmon clutched in its talons. In summer, golden-crowned kinglets call from the trees, swallows dive for insects, and dippers bob along the river banks like tireless windup toys.

Running a course straighter than the Cedar River, the trail takes you alternately from forest to riverside to bridge. About 1 mile from Landsburg Park (the easternmost trailhead), a reconstructed 1908 railroad bridge spans the river. High above the water, you have an eagle's-eye view both up- and downstream to cliffs, eddies, and rapids. From here, you can loop back to Landsburg by exploring the sandy path that traces the river's edge. Search the ground for prints and droppings of deer and elk. Imagine the coyote, cougar, and bobcat hunting their prey.

Alternatively, continue west as long as your feet and time hold out: several hours gets you to the underpass of SR 18 and SR 169. At this point, the trail loses its appeal as it borders the Maple Valley Highway for several miles. See Walk #66, Cedar River Trail (northwest section) for another lovely stretch of this trail.

*How to Get There:* From I-90 east of Bellevue, eastbound, take exit 17 (Front St, Issaquah). Turn right (south) on Front St which becomes the Issaquah-Hobart Rd. Go 3 miles past Hobart to Landsburg Park on the Cedar River. The trail begins on the right (west) side.

From I-405 in Renton north- or southbound, take exit 4 (SR 169, Maple Valley, Enumclaw). Go south on SR 169 (Maple Valley Hwy) 10 miles to Maple Valley. Go under SR 18, turn left onto SE 216th Way. Park here for one end of the trail (walk behind the Testy Chef Cafe to the river). OR continue east on SE 216th Way which becomes SE 216th St. Go 3 miles and turn right onto 276th Ave SE (Issaquah-Hobart Road). Go 2.4 miles to Landsburg Park (just before the Cedar River crossing). Trail begins on the west side of the road.

From I-5 north of Tacoma, north- or southbound, take exit 142A (SR 18 east to Auburn, North Bend) and go east on SR 18 to SR 516. Go east on SR 516. 1.2 miles after passing SR 169 turn left (north) on Landsburg Rd SE. Go 1.5 miles to Landsburg Park. Alternatively, stay on SR 18 to the SR 169 (Renton, Maple Valley) exit. At the end of the ramp, take a right on SE 231st St, then turn left (north) on SR 169 toward Renton and Maple Valley. Go about 0.8 mile, cross the Cedar River and park where possible near the corner of SR 169 and SE 216th Way. (Access is behind the Testy Chef Cafe.) King County Parks (206) 296-4281.

# #69
# SOUTH KING COUNTY ARBORETUM

MAPLE VALLEY, 22 MILES SOUTHEAST OF BELLEVUE

| | |
|---|---|
| HIGHLIGHTS | *Native and exotic plants, forest, bird-watching* |
| TRAIL | *2.5 miles total; gravel and natural surfaces* |
| OTHER USAGE | *Pedestrians only on nature loop; horses* |
| STEEPNESS | *Level (garden) to moderate (forest)* |
| CONNECTING TRAILS | *Lake Wilderness Trail* |
| PARK SERVICES | *Nature trail brochure and map, guided walks by arrangement, classes, plant sales* |
| DISABLED ACCESS | *Garden trails* |

IN ONE WALK YOU CAN ENJOY BOTH AN ORNAMENTAL GARDEN OF NATIVE plants and a natural second-growth forest typical of Cascade foothills. The South King County Arboretum Foundation, a nonprofit volunteer group, has created these gardens to provide examples of native plants and to teach the importance of choosing non-native ornamental plants that will thrive here without extra water or fertilizer. On the garden trails you can see a wide variety of rhododendrons, both species and hybrids, and showy trees such as the purple-leafed smoke tree and unusual maples. Spring is, of course, spectacular with color, but each season offers some new and colorful changes in the garden. Volunteers are needed—there are always more plantings and projects in the works.

Across the old railroad grade (part of the Lake Wilderness Trail) you enter a mature second-growth forest. On the Self-guided Loop you can read about and observe this transitional forest, in which the more shade-tolerant western hemlocks and western red cedars are slowly replacing the Douglas firs. From high in the canopy secretive warblers sing, and tiny brown creepers spiral their way up the trunks in search of bark-dwelling insects. Orange lichen paints intriguing patterns on the trunks of the bigleaf maples.

*How to Get There:* From I-5 north of Tacoma, north- or southbound, take exit 142A (SR 18 east to Auburn, North Bend). Follow SR 18 east to the SR 169 exit. At the end of the ramp, turn right on SE 231st St, then right (south) on SR 169. Go 0.3 mile and turn right again (south) on Witte Rd. Go 0.8 mile and turn left on SE 248th St. The Arboretum is at 0.5 mile, just before the entrance to Lake Wilderness County Park (services available there).

From I-405 in Renton north- or southbound, take exit 4 (SR 169, Maple Valley). Turn east (right if northbound, left and under the freeway if southbound). Go 10 miles on SR 169 to Maple Valley. After crossing SR 18, turn right on Witte Rd and proceed as above. King County Parks (206) 296-4281.

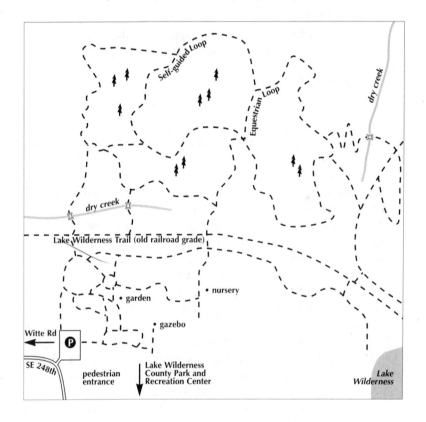

# #70
# SOOS CREEK TRAIL

KENT, 19 MILES SOUTH OF BELLEVUE, 21 MILES NORTHEAST OF TACOMA

| | |
|---|---|
| HIGHLIGHTS | *Stream, wetlands, forest, bird-watching* |
| TRAIL | *4.5 miles one way; paved* |
| OTHER USAGE | *Bicycles, horses; horses sometimes on separate trail* |
| STEEPNESS | *Level to gentle* |
| CONNECTING TRAILS | *None* |
| PARK SERVICES | *Restrooms, picnic tables, brochure, interpretive walks May through September (206) 296-4171* |
| DISABLED ACCESS | *Restrooms and trail* |

JUST INCHES ABOVE THE MARSHES, THE PATH CUTS A STRAIGHT DARK line through one of the finest wetlands in King County. Chickadees call *chicka dee dee dee* from the branches of alder and oak. A red-tailed hawk soars overhead. Soos Creek Trail is a walker's hidden paradise just minutes from downtown Kent.

Marshes like this one have an all-season appeal. In summer the trail is busy with skaters, bicycles, and walkers, and the marsh plants are tall and thick with green stalks and golden brown cattails. The landscape feels enclosed and intimate. In winter the wet meadow areas predominate, with hardhack, alder, willow, and many bird species. In winter, too, you can see through the brush to the hillsides of fir and hemlock that rise from the creek.

The park's shape is defined by meandering Soos Creek. Along the length of the trail you pass through several distinct types of wetlands. Ponds are home to great blue herons, ducks, geese, cattails, rushes, skunk cabbage, and wild roses. Scrub wetlands remain flooded year-round. In the forested wetland you'll walk beside vine maple, cedar, salmonberry, and elderberry; then you climb to the upland forest, with its second-growth cedars, maples, and ferns.

Originally owned by the Northern Pacific Railroad, the land was logged at the turn of the century by large timber companies. After that,

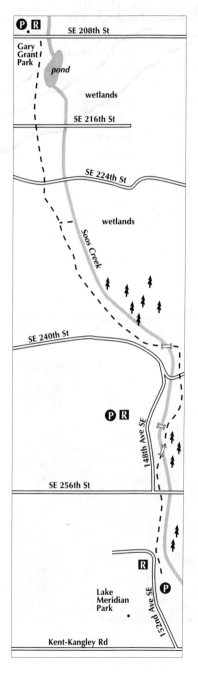

Finnish pioneers arrived, clearing the land with oxen and horses to raise fruits and vegetables. Look for remnants of the old orchards along the trail.

*How to Get There:* To reach the southern trailhead: From I-5 south of Seattle, northbound, take exit 149A (SR 516, Kent). Southbound, take exit 149 (SR 516, Kent). Head east on SR 516 toward Kent. After crossing under SR 167 go 5.7 miles on SR 516 making the following turns: straight on Willis St, left on 4th Ave, right on Smith St, across Central Ave where it becomes Canyon Dr SE then SE 256th St, finally becoming Kent-Kangley Rd (just after the light on 104th Ave SE). After passing Lake Meridian, turn left (north) at the light on 152nd Ave SE. Parking and trailhead are on the right.

To reach the northern trailhead: From I-405 in Renton, north- or southbound, take exit 2 (SR 167 south, Auburn). Go 3.9 miles and turn left (east) on SE 212th St. Go 3 miles (SE 212th St becomes SE 208th St) to Gary Grant Park. King County Parks (206) 296-4281.

# #71
# DES MOINES BEACH PARK

**DES MOINES, ON PUGET SOUND, 14 MILES SOUTH OF SEATTLE,
15 MILES NORTH OF TACOMA**

| | |
|---:|:---|
| HIGHLIGHTS | *Saltwater beach, stream, bird-watching* |
| TRAIL | *1 mile one way, including half-mile marina walk; paved and natural surfaces* |
| OTHER USAGE | *Bicycles* |
| STEEPNESS | *Level; one steep trail* |
| CONNECTING TRAILS | *None* |
| PARK SERVICES | *Restrooms, picnic shelters, playground, senior center, classes; Des Moines Marina, fishing pier* |
| DISABLED ACCESS | *Restrooms, paved trail, marina facilities* |

SURF SCOTERS, GOLDENEYES, AND GREBES DABBLE, PADDLE, AND MUCK about in the food-rich soup of salt and fresh water. Gulls call *cheer, cheer*

Low tide at Des Moines Beach Park exposes a feast for waterfowl

and squabble over clams. Inland, the forest beckons with cool shade or the sound of water on its last burbling yards to the sea.

Touted as one of King County's prime bird-watching sites, this small park is truly alive with avian creatures. Along the shore you may see kingfishers and eagles as well as the waterfowl. Though the walks are not long, they have diversity. A short, steep training walk up the northern hill leads to neighborhoods. A gentle stroll through the old grounds of the church camp (now a community center, senior center, and picnic shelter) borders clear, shallow Des Moines Creek. Follow the broken

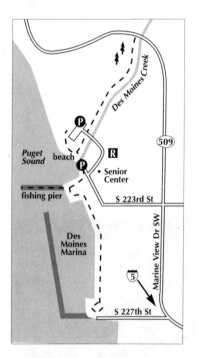

pavement of the old road farther east to a wooded grotto where the creek pours from a culvert.

For an extended walk head south along the waterfront and public marina, where green gives way to blue: blue Sound (if you're lucky), and blue and white boats.

*How to Get There:* **From I-5 south of Seattle, northbound, take exit 149B (SR 516 west to Kent). Southbound, take exit 149. Go 2 miles west on the Kent-Des Moines Rd (SR 516), and merge right into Marine View Dr S. Go about 5 blocks and turn left on S 223rd St. This drops down the hill becoming Cliff St which enters the park. Additional parking is available at the south end of the Marina. Des Moines Parks (206) 870-6527.**

# #72
# SALTWATER STATE PARK

## On Puget Sound, 14 miles north of Tacoma

| | |
|---|---|
| HIGHLIGHTS | *Tide pools, beach, views, forest, salmon-spawning stream* |
| TRAIL | *2 miles total; natural surface* |
| OTHER USAGE | *Bicycles* |
| STEEPNESS | *Level to steep* |
| CONNECTING TRAILS | *None* |
| PARK SERVICES | *Restrooms, picnic areas, camping, underwater park, concession stand (summer only)* |
| DISABLED ACCESS | *Restrooms, picnic areas, camping* |

At low tide 1,500 feet of rocky beach creates a multitude of tide pools. Here red and yellow starfish cling, crabs scuttle, and snails creep. Inland, cool shaded forest lets you wander over a hillside and to a bluff overlooking the Sound and seagoing vessels.

**Palm-sized oyster shells are a common sight on Puget Sound beaches**

One of the most popular state parks on Puget Sound, Saltwater sees upwards of three-quarters of a million visitors a year. The nice thing is, they mostly come in summer and on warm weekends and most of them visit the beach. With careful timing you can be virtually alone on the beach, communing with clams and mussels or watching the antics of the seagulls and crows as they drop the mollusks from the air to the concrete for an instant breakfast. At high tide, walk the several hundred yards of paved walkway next to the riprap bulkhead right on the water.

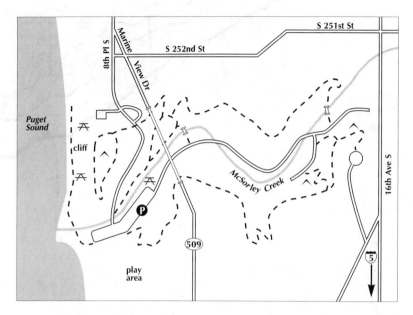

For a forest stroll, leave from the playground and follow the soft-sur-faced path along the hillside under a mix of Douglas fir and bigleaf maple. This forest was last logged about 60 years ago, and the second-growth trees are reaching a hefty size. The lush undergrowth helps to muffle the sounds of visitors and the hum of traffic on the bridge over-head. The trail loops back to the McSorley Creek ravine at the eastern end of the campground. Other trails lead from the valley, make loops, and return. On the north side of the camping area a footbridge crosses McSorley Creek, which once again sees a salmon run.

*How to Get There:* From I-5 south of Seattle, north- or southbound, take exit 147 (S 272nd St). Go west (right if southbound, left if northbound) on S 272nd St about 0.75 mile to 16th Ave S. Turn right on 16th Ave S and watch for State Park signs that lead to the park. Washington State Parks (800) 233-0321.

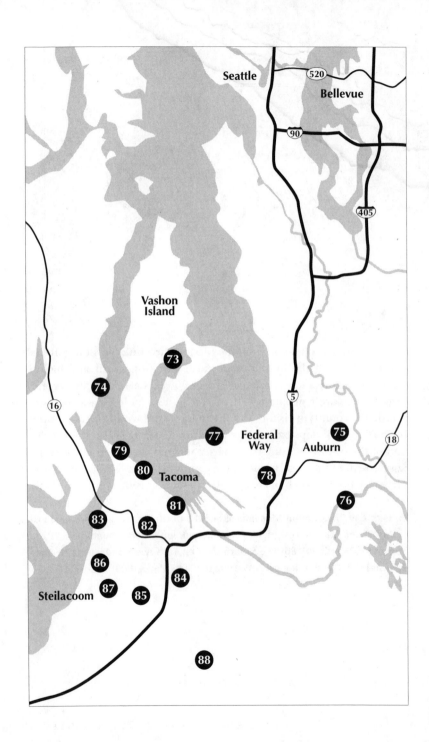

# IN AND AROUND TACOMA

# #73
# BURTON ACRES PARK

VASHON ISLAND, ON PUGET SOUND, 14 MILES NORTH OF TACOMA
(INCLUDING FERRY)

| | |
|---|---|
| HIGHLIGHTS | *Mature forest, waterfront* |
| TRAIL | *1.1-mile loop, including center trails; natural surface* |
| OTHER USAGE | *Bicycles* |
| STEEPNESS | *Gentle* |
| CONNECTING TRAILS | *None* |
| PARK SERVICES | *Restrooms, boat launch, picnic tables* |
| DISABLED ACCESS | *Restrooms* |

ENTER A FOREST CATHEDRAL, ALMOST A CENTURY OLD. THE DEEPLY furrowed bark of the old Douglas firs leads your eyes upwards. Between the pillarlike trunks, neat clusters of sword fern and Oregon grape are arranged like offerings. Walk silently on paths filled with fir needles. The bigleaf maples grow multiple trunks like candelabras.

Saved from the enthusiasm of 19th-century farmers for burning stumps and clearing acreage, these 68 acres belonged to Miles Hatch, a Tacoma businessman who started a college at Burton, where he pioneered in the late 1800's. Although the park has a small beach, picnic area, and boat launch, its allure lies in the forest. Enter it from either of two paths that lead from Burton Road across from the boat launch. By turning right every time the trail splits, you can experiment with making a loop. If you find that your choice has led you to a house, retrace your steps to the junction and take the other path.

The northern section has an open and spacious feel. The squat stumps with their rectangular springboard holes look like sylvan dwarves in a Disney cartoon. Fallen giant trees show the shallow root system of the Douglas firs and how easily they are uprooted in winter windstorms. As you take the loop trail, you'll notice subtle changes. In the western section, English ivy has invaded from the bordering neighborhoods, threatening to engulf the shrubbery and stumps. The brush, too, is higher, composed of blackberry and nettle, and the trees trunks are smaller. A gentle decline in the trail takes you back into the past, back into the cathedral of older trees.

*How to Get There:* From West Seattle (Fauntleroy) take the ferry to Southworth (Vashon Island). Go south on Vashon Hwy SW about 8.8 miles. Turn left on Burton Dr, follow it to the north and around the peninsula. Look on the left for a boat launch and park sign. The trail begins across the street to the right.

From Tacoma (Pt. Defiance) take the ferry to Tahlequah (Vashon Island). Go north on Vashon Hwy SW about 5.5 miles. Turn right on Burton Dr and follow it to the north and around the peninsula. Proceed as above. Vashon Island Parks (206) 463-9602.

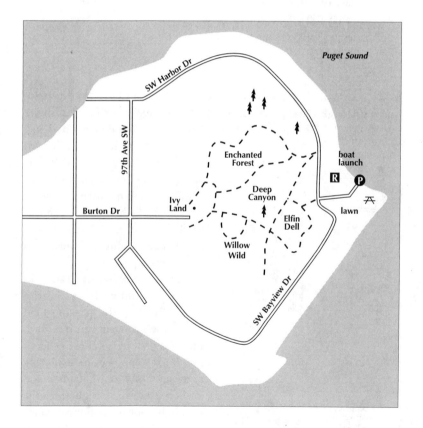

# #74
# SUNRISE BEACH PARK

| | |
|---|---|
| HIGHLIGHTS | *Saltwater beach, Mount Rainier views, forest* |
| TRAIL | *1.5 miles total; beach and natural surface* |
| OTHER USAGE | *Pedestrians only* |
| STEEPNESS | *Gentle to steep* |
| CONNECTING TRAILS | *None* |
| PARK SERVICES | *Restrooms* |
| DISABLED ACCESS | *None* |

STROLL A FOREST PATH UNDER MOSS-COVERED BIGLEAF MAPLES AND 80-year-old Douglas firs, or climb a steep trail to small clearings that single out Mount Rainier and water views. This neighborhood beach park just

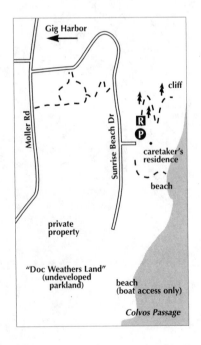

outside Gig Harbor is a tiny gem tucked away in a back-roads part of Pierce County. A gift from two families, the park forms a patchwork along Colvos Passage and its southern portion, 30 acres of old forest, beach, and wetlands, is as yet undeveloped.

For the viewpoint trail and beach, continue down Sunrise Beach Road to the parking field from which you can venture down the grassy slope to the tree-lined beach for some low-tide exploring and views of Mount Rainier and Vashon Island. At high tide, the beach disappears, and waves make a song of water on wood as they lap and slap against the wooden sea wall.

To hike the steep, viewpoint trail, return to the parking field and look on the north side against the hill for the trailhead sign. After you run the prickly, stinging gauntlet of blackberry and nettle, the trail widens and a lush green forest encircles you. A massive bigleaf maple with multiple trunks borders the steeply climbing trail. Not for the faint of heart or for young children, the now-narrow path ascends along the side of a steep ravine to the first of several viewpoints. Summer foliage masks Rainier but allows tempting glimpses of the water and Vashon far below. At the second viewpoint, the scene widens and the water shimmers beneath the cliff. Circling the hill, the trail traverses high above a few homes, past old stumps with crevices that house shrews and mice. A wooden sign and an abrupt bluff declare the trail's end. Here, at last, you have a clear, inspiring view of Mount Rainier.

It's best to avoid this trail in wet weather because of its steep, hill-hugging ascent. But try it in fair weather and be rewarded with late-afternoon sunglow on the mountain.

For the gentle forest loop, look for trailheads (with limited parking) on both Moller Road and Sunrise Beach Road.

*How to Get There:* From I-5 in Tacoma, north- or southbound, take exit 132 (SR 16 west, Gig Harbor). Follow SR 16 west over the Tacoma Narrows Bridge. After the bridge go 3.7 miles to Gig Harbor and take the Pioneer Way exit. Go to the T junction at Harborview Dr and turn left, staying on Harborview as it veers right, hugging the water. At the T junction with Vernhardson St, turn right. Go to Crescent Valley Dr NW and turn left. Go 0.6 mile and turn right on Drummond Dr (Crescent Valley cut off). Go 0.8 mile to the T junction at Moller Dr NW. Jog right, then left onto Sunrise Beach Rd at the Sunrise Beach Park sign. The road is narrow and winding. Pierce County Parks (206) 593-4176.

# #75
# ISAAC EVANS PARK

**AUBURN, ON THE GREEN RIVER, 18 MILES NORTHEAST OF TACOMA**

| | |
|---|---|
| HIGHLIGHTS | *River* |
| TRAIL | *1 mile round trip; paved* |
| OTHER USAGE | *Bicycles* |
| STEEPNESS | *Level* |
| CONNECTING TRAILS | *None* |
| PARK SERVICES | *Restrooms, playground, picnic shelters* |
| DISABLED ACCESS | *Restrooms, trail* |

JUST 6 MILES INLAND AS THE NORTHWEST RAVEN FLIES, THE GREEN River makes its final push north toward its juncture with the Duwamish River and Elliott Bay. After flowing among meadows and forests, it enters the urban areas still clear and energetic, shallow and inviting. Although the City of Auburn and King County have set aside a longer swath of riverside parkland, the best walking and viewing are currently at tiny Isaac Evans Park.

Paved trails (all fully accessible) criss-cross and form loops across the neat lawns. Start at either the north or the south end, and stroll the park. Black cottonwoods line the riverbank, with snowberries creating a decorative skirt around each trunk. Young hemlock and cedar add year-round greenery. In places the brushy bank gives way to a sandy slope. Here the flooding river deposited sand and then receded, its normal current not strong enough or high enough to reclaim the sand. Watch for migrating waterfowl paddling the river.

**Sharing the Trail with Bikes:**

*Bicycles are required to yield to pedestrians, but they still seem to appear from nowhere, usually from behind. On a multiuse trail, stay to the right, or just off the pavement on the right. Be prepared for a sudden voice saying "On the left," indicating that someone is about to pass you on your left. Teach kids to walk on the right and not to dart across the path.*

At the southern end a picturesque suspension bridge spans the river, leading to a smaller neighborhood park and playground.

*How to Get There:* **From I-5 north of Tacoma, north- or southbound, take exit 142A (SR 18 east, Auburn). Go 4 miles and exit at SR 164, looping around under the freeway and back north. Go right on E Main St, left on "N" St NE, and then right onto Henry Rd. After crossing the river, take a left on Riverside Ave which becomes Green River Rd. Go 1 mile. The park is on the left.**

**From I-405 near Renton, north- or southbound, take exit 2 (SR 167 south, Auburn). Go 6.7 miles south to SR 516 (Willis St) exit. Turn east (left) on W Willis St and go straight through Kent. At the T junction against a wooded hillside, take a right onto Central. Take the first left (S 259th St) which veers right to become Green River Rd. Go about 3.5 miles south on Green River Rd to the park across from the Auburn Golf Course. Auburn Parks (206) 931-3043.**

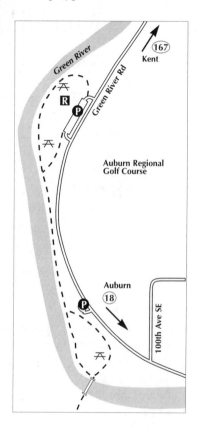

# #76

# GAME FARM AND GAME FARM WILDERNESS PARKS

### Auburn, 17 miles northeast of Tacoma

| | |
|---|---|
| HIGHLIGHTS | *Glacier-fed river* |
| TRAIL | *4 miles total; paved and natural surfaces* |
| OTHER USAGE | *Bicycles* |
| STEEPNESS | *Level* |
| CONNECTING TRAILS | *None* |
| PARK SERVICES | *Restrooms, picnic shelters, playing fields, playgrounds, sports courts, campgrounds* |
| DISABLED ACCESS | *Restrooms, picnic shelters, amphitheater, 2 miles of paved trail in Game Farm Park, campgrounds and short paved trail in Wilderness Park* |

THESE NONIDENTICAL TWIN PARKS LINE BOTH SIDES OF THE MILKY, glacially fed White River (which becomes the Stuck River as it passes the parks). Here you can choose civilization, amenities, and landscaping at Game Farm Park on the north, or a wilder, less gentrified park on the south.

Game Farm Park (named for its past history as a site on which shooting stock was raised) throbs with activity. Colonnades of landscaping trees border playing fields that are interconnected with over 2 miles of paved walkways. Come for people-watching on weekends, and for solitude on damp winter days. Park near the amphitheater at the southern end and walk past the picnic shelters toward the river. The almost-century-old diversion dam divides park landscaping from river wilderness. Walk along it, or step over it to find an unmaintained but well-used path on the riverbank. Follow this path of sand and rounded river rocks east along the river. Side trails lead to possible wading and picnic areas on the shores. (See note on rivers, page 75.) Beaver-toppled trees, with their telltale gnawing marks, lie jumbled in the river, awaiting removal by the rodents or the next flood.

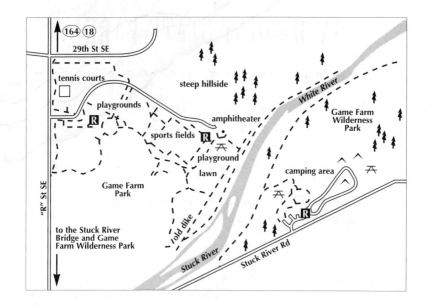

Across the river in Game Farm Wilderness Park, an RV campground, restrooms, and picnic shelters are the only amenities. Again, a natural sand-and-rock path leads east along the river with access points for fishing or wading. Watch for dippers—small brown birds that bob and hunt for food along the rocky rapids. Breathe deeply of this fresh river-scented air. Across the water 150-foot-high bluffs are a geological window to the past, while today's trees cling tenaciously to the sandy walls. West from the day-use area, a short paved trail invites walkers, baby strollers, and wheelchairs.

*How to Get There:* From I-5 north of Tacoma, north- or southbound, take exit 142A (SR 18 east, Auburn). Go 4 miles and exit at SR 164 (Auburn Way). Head south staying on the lower part of the road (Howard Rd). Turn right onto "R" St and go south 13 blocks to Game Farm Park on your left. The Wilderness Park is farther south on "R" St, just across the river, also on your left.

From I-405 near Renton, north- or southbound, take exit 2 (SR 167 south, Auburn). Go about 10 miles south to SR 18. Go east (left) on SR 18 to the SR 164 (Auburn Way) exit and proceed as above. Auburn Parks (206) 931-3043.

#77

# DASH POINT STATE PARK

FEDERAL WAY, ON PUGET SOUND, 13 MILES NORTH OF TACOMA

| | |
|---|---|
| HIGHLIGHTS | *Saltwater beach, forest* |
| TRAIL | *7.5 miles total; natural surface* |
| OTHER USAGE | *Pedestrians only* |
| STEEPNESS | *Level to steep* |
| CONNECTING TRAILS | *None* |
| PARK SERVICES | *Restrooms, picnic shelters, camping* |
| DISABLED ACCESS | *Restrooms* |

THE SNOW-COVERED PEAKS OF THE OLYMPICS JUT INTO THE ICE-BLUE sky to the west. Bald eagles glide, or beat their wings against the winter wind, holding place over the whitecaps of the water. Seagulls screech and harass the eagles for a share of the meal. Bold and dramatic, this is the Sound in winter seen from the wind-whipped beach at Dash Point.

But whatever the season, the low-tide beach is always inviting with its long strolls (3,300 feet each way) along firm and rippled sand. Views are fine across the East Passage to Maury Island, Vashon Island, and the Olympics. On hot summer weekends, the beach area is crowded with families and children. Driftwood, adorned in black and silver mussel shells and rosettes of barnacles, accents the gently sloping beach. To the north, where the park hillsides pitch steeply to the beach, fir and madrona trees lie across the sand, their roots torn loose from the hill. But at low tide, you can skirt these and walk until your calves ache.

**Nature's sculpting: red madrona bark**

To escape the crowds or the rising tide, head inland for quiet forest walks. From the southeastern corner of the beach parking lot, a dirt-and-sand trail pursues the creek under high maples, firs, and red alders. These miles of trail are for worry-free wandering—some lead nowhere, some to campground loops. Sturdy wooden bridges span the stream, and steps with railings ease the steep climb from beach to bluff.

*How to Get There:* From I-5 north of Tacoma, north- or southbound, take exit 143, (Federal Way, S 320th St). Turn west (left if northbound, right if southbound) on S 320th St. Go about 4.7 miles and turn right (north) on 47th Ave SW. At the next T junction turn left onto Dash Point Rd (SR 509). The park entrance is on the right in about 0.5 mile. Washington State Parks (800) 233-0321.

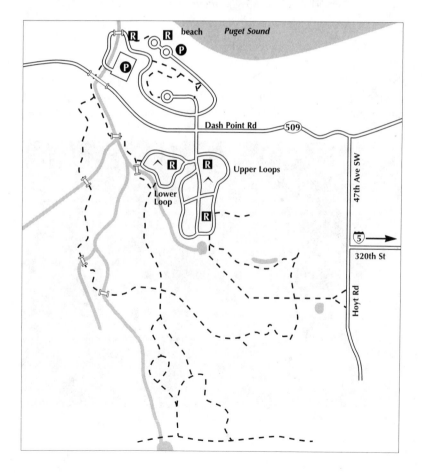

# #78
# WEST HYLEBOS WETLANDS STATE PARK

**FEDERAL WAY, 11.5 MILES NORTHEAST OF TACOMA**

| | |
|---|---|
| HIGHLIGHTS | *Wetlands, forest, bird-watching* |
| TRAIL | *1-mile loop; boardwalk* |
| OTHER USAGE | *Pedestrians only; no pets* |
| STEEPNESS | *Level* |
| CONNECTING TRAILS | *None* |
| PARK SERVICES | *Restrooms, interpretive trail* |
| DISABLED ACCESS | *Restrooms, trail* |

NESTLED IN THE HEART OF FEDERAL WAY, THIS SMALL ENCLAVE OF NATIVE wetland is a schoolroom in the wild. Rich, earthy scents accompany you along the dry, boardwalked trail. Interpretive markers call attention to

Vine maple leaves on an algae-covered wetland

wetlands plants and common inhabitants of the peat bog and stream bank. The walkways "float" on a cushioning of 36 feet of peat that dates back 12,000 to 15,000 years. Moss drapes heavily from the limbs of the bigleaf maples.

This park has caught the attention of environmental groups, researchers, and nature enthusiasts alike. But the main thrust of interest in the park has come from octogenarian Ilene Marckx, whose home adjoins the park. She, together with her late husband, Francis, donated about 25 acres to the State in the late 1980s with the dream of creating a wetlands preserve.

Birds, although not easy to see because of the dense vegetation and the low light, raise their voices in a chorus of song in the early morning and serenade the sunset. Hawks and other birds of prey frequent the park and its surroundings. Great blue herons feed at Mar Lake as though it were a breakfast buffet.

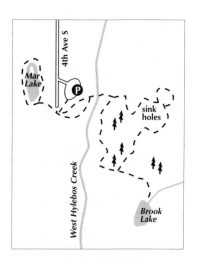

Don't plan to visit Hylebos immediately after a heavy winter storm; the stream floods about three times each winter, prohibiting access to Brook Lake and leaving the boardwalks slippery. Call for conditions.

*How to Get There:* **From I-5 north of Tacoma, northbound, take exit 142B (SR 99, Federal Way). If southbound, take exit 142B (SR 161 south, Puyallup, Federal Way). Turn west (left if northbound, right if southbound) on S 348th St toward Federal Way. Go 0.5 mile and cross Pacific Hwy. In another 0.5 mile turn left onto 4th Ave S (just past St. Francis Hospital). The park is signposted here. Go 2 blocks to the parking lot. Washington State Parks (800) 233-0321.**

# #79
# POINT DEFIANCE PARK

TACOMA, ON PUGET SOUND, 5 MILES NORTHWEST OF DOWNTOWN

| | |
|---|---|
| HIGHLIGHTS | *Forest, Olympic views, saltwater beach, gardens, art, historical site* |
| TRAIL | *8 miles total; paved, gravel, and natural surfaces* |
| OTHER USAGE | *Pedestrians only in forest; no bicycles except on paved trails* |
| STEEPNESS | *Level to steep* |
| CONNECTING TRAILS | *None* |
| PARK SERVICES | *Restrooms, picnic shelters, beach, gardens (zoo, aquarium, logging museum, children's entertainment - admission fee)* |
| DISABLED ACCESS | *The Promenade (1 mile, Owen Beach to Boathouse Marina), park facilities (sawdust-covered trails in Never Never Land)* |

IT WOULD BE HARD TO CHOSE ONE TRAIL ABOVE ALL OTHERS IN THIS 700-acre park on the northwest tip of Tacoma. Whatever your pleasure in walking trails, you'll find it here. Near the main entrance at Park Avenue and Pearl Street, paved trails circulate throughout the formal park zone with its pond and gardens. Explore the world-class Rose Garden, the Japanese Garden and, for a steeper walk, the Native Garden. Stroll the paved Promenade from the boathouse to Owen Beach. On Five-Mile Drive the Rhododendron Garden, ablaze with color in the early spring, leads to more wooded paths. High in the interior of the park, a ridge trail, bisecting the park through its wild old forest, provides quiet on natural trails and an intimacy with nature not found near the beach and picnic areas.

For water views, try the walk north from the Vashon Viewpoint (on Five-Mile Drive). This wooded trail passes wondrous old Douglas firs, cedars, and hemlocks. The earthen path muffles sounds, and as the trail curves farther from the road, the silence settles around you. Because of the age of this forest (almost 100 years), the undergrowth is sparse and a carpet of needles lies on the forest floor. Go past the footpath to the beach, continuing until you come to the immense Mountaineer Tree. This Douglas fir, the largest living tree in the park, measures 218 feet tall and is over 400 years old. If it survives nature (and human vandalism), it could still be standing 500 years from now.

*How to Get There:* From I-5 in Tacoma, north- or southbound, take exit 132 (SR 16 west, Gig Harbor, Bremerton). Go 3.6 miles to the 6th Ave/Pearl St exit. Turn left (west) on 6th Ave, then right (north) on Pearl St/SR 163. Go north 3 miles on Pearl St which ends at the Point Defiance Park entrance. On Saturday mornings Five-Mile Dr is closed to motorized vehicles but other access points are open. Metropolitan Park District of Tacoma (206) 305-1000.

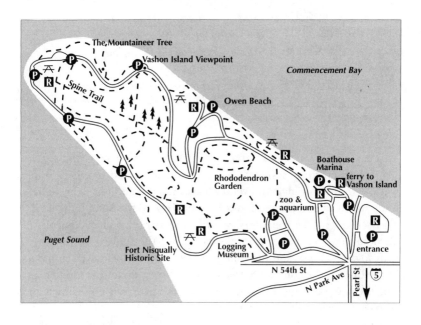

# #80
# RUSTON WAY WATERFRONT AND PUGET GARDENS

TACOMA, ON PUGET SOUND, 2.5 MILES NORTHWEST OF DOWNTOWN

HIGHLIGHTS *Saltwater beach, Mount Rainier views, garden, stream, art*

TRAIL *2.5 miles one way on waterfront, paved. Garden is gravel, 0.5 mile*

OTHER USAGE *Bicycles. Garden is pedestrians only.*

STEEPNESS *Level*

CONNECTING TRAILS *Puget Creek Habitat restoration trail*

PARK SERVICES *Restrooms, picnic tables, fishing pier, restored fireboat*

DISABLED ACCESS *Restrooms, picnic areas, fishing pier, paved trail; none in Puget Gardens*

FOR TWO AND A HALF MILES ALONG COMMENCEMENT BAY, A LANDSCAPED strip of green grass connects parks, restaurants, and beaches. Maple trees, with their orange and yellow leaves in fall and their delicate bare branches in winter, frame Mount Rainier. Toward the Sound, the view is always changing as freighters, yachts, and barges pull in and out of Tacoma's busy harbor and kayaks dart along the shore. On the beach, drift logs lie about, and old pilings and concrete blocks are reminders of the once-active commercial waterfront. Now gulls and sandpipers patrol the water's edge. Evening light pours warm sun on Rainier and turns the bay to gold and crimson.

To reach Puget Gardens, turn inland on Alder Street, about midway along Ruston Way, and follow it one block to the corner of Lawrence and Alder. Here tiny Puget Gardens nestles at the base of Puget Gulch. Originally created and tended by the Skupen family, the park is now under the care of volunteers and school children, whose ceramic art is showcased here. Native plants and ornamentals lend color and texture to the pathways. The stream is banked with logs to make ponds suitable for salmon spawning, and carefully placed rocks orchestrate the water music as the stream flows toward Commencement Bay.

*How to Get There:* From I-5 in Tacoma, north- or southbound, take exit 133 (I-705 north, City Center). Follow signs for Schuster Pkwy which becomes Ruston Way. The walking trail links several parks along Ruston Way, beginning with Commencement Park at the southern end. Park here and walk north or park at any of the designated lots along Ruston Way. To reach Puget Gardens, turn off Ruston Way onto N Alder St. There is on-street parking for only 2 cars by Puget Gardens. Metropolitan Park District of Tacoma (206) 305-1000.

Crowded Trails? *You can help the congestion. Choose to walk in less-than-perfect weather. Walk at times other than lunch hours or weekend afternoons. Encourage bicycling friends to contact the Cascade Bicycle Club (206) 522-BIKE to get ideas on where to bike away from pedestrians.*

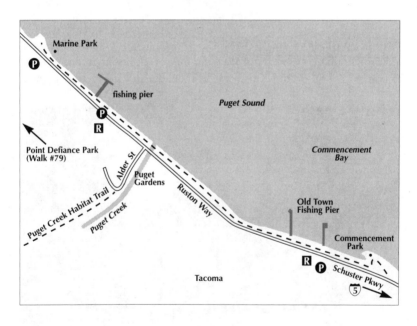

# #81
# WRIGHT PARK

**TACOMA, DOWNTOWN**

| | |
|---|---|
| HIGHLIGHTS | *Conservatory, arboretum, pond, art* |
| TRAIL | *1.5 miles total; gravel* |
| OTHER USAGE | *Bicycles* |
| STEEPNESS | *Level to gentle* |
| CONNECTING TRAILS | *None* |
| PARK SERVICES | *Restrooms, picnic tables, horseshoe pits, putting green, lawn bowling, wading pool, playground, community center, classes* |
| DISABLED ACCESS | *Restrooms, community center, conservatory, paths* |

MOIST, WARM AIR AWAKENS THE SENSE OF SMELL, AND BRILLIANT FLORAL colors stimulate eyes weary of Washington's ever-present green. Birds of paradise, exotic orchids, tropical bromeliads, and poinsettias paint a

**Seymour Conservatory promises year-round color in Wright Park**

wild palette of color inside the Seymour Conservatory. Outside, exotic trees from Asia and Europe add new and unfamiliar forms to the lawns etched by zigzagging paths.

A patch of elegant greenery in historic Tacoma, this 100-year-old park is unique in its spacious landscaping. Follow the paths up and down gentle hillocks. Pause to watch the antics of the mallards on the pond or feel the emotion created by sculptor Larry Anderson's *The Leaf*, south of the community center. But people, more than plants, animals, and art, are the focus of this lively park. As you walk, watch the gyrations of intense young basketball players, the graceful moves of the lawn bowlers, the directed concentration of the horseshoe players. Then carry on your walk—there are lots of tree species to learn.

***How to Get There:*** From I-5 in Tacoma, north-or southbound, take exit 132 (SR 16 west, Gig Harbor, Bremerton). From SR 16 take the first exit, Sprague Ave, and go 1.5 miles to S 6th Ave. Turn right (east) on S 6th Ave to S "I" St and the park. Curbside parking around the park. Conservatory open daily 10-4:30, free admission. Metropolitan Park District of Tacoma (206) 305-1000.

# #82
# THE NATURE CENTER AT SNAKE LAKE

TACOMA, 3 MILES WEST OF DOWNTOWN

| | |
|---|---|
| HIGHLIGHTS | *Lake, wetlands, forest, bird-watching* |
| TRAIL | *1-mile Wetland Loop, 1.5-mile Hilltop Forest Loop; natural surface* |
| OTHER USAGE | *Pedestrians only* |
| STEEPNESS | *Level to moderate* |
| CONNECTING TRAILS | *None* |
| PARK SERVICES | *Restrooms, interpretive center, classes, interpretive trail* |
| DISABLED ACCESS | *Restrooms and interpretive center* |

THE FOREST HERE SEEMS INTIMATE, AS THOUGH NATURE WERE WRAPPING you in earth and lake smells, vine and shrub textures, and the songs of birds. Ten feet from the trail and indifferent to human presence, the wood ducks continue pecking and grooming on the muddy bank of Snake Lake. Each line of their vivid poster-colored heads stands out in sharp contrast to the brown earth.

Winter is a rewarding time to visit this small snake-shaped lake in the midst of commercial Tacoma. Where only a corner of water remains unfrozen, the ducks, geese, and grebes congregate in massive displays of color and motion. The snowberry and blackberry thickets stand crisp and naked without their greenery, letting you watch the wrens flit from twig to twig.

**All Five Senses:** *Walking is a sensory experience. Teach kids to look, listen, touch, smell and taste. Teach them the difference between edible and nonedible berries right away, and between touchable and untouchable plants. Be sure you know which is which.*

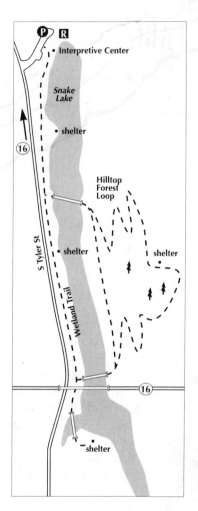

Warmer weather, though, invites you to explore all 54 acres. Walk the Wetland Loop, with a stop or two on the bridges or in the wildlife blinds along the trail, to see what creatures come to feed among the reeds. Year-round waterfowl include mallards, Canada geese, and wood ducks. A climb up the Hilltop Forest Loop above the lake promises more exercise and the refreshing cool of shade. Early-morning visitors may see prints of the resident red foxes.

The Nature Center has displays, hands-on activities for both adults and kids, interpretive information, and a gift shop.

***How to Get There:*** **From I-5 in Tacoma, north- or southbound, take exit 132 (SR 16 west, Gig Harbor, Bremerton). Go 2.5 miles and take the 19th St east exit. Turn right on 19th St then right again on S Tyler St. Trails are open 8 AM to dusk daily. The interpretive center is open Mon-Sat, 8 AM to 5 PM (206) 591-6439. Metropolitan Park District of Tacoma (206) 305-1000.**

# #83
# TITLOW PARK

**TACOMA, ON THE NARROWS, 5 MILES WEST OF DOWNTOWN**

| | |
|---|---|
| HIGHLIGHTS | *Saltwater beach, Olympic views, forest, lagoon, wetlands* |
| TRAIL | *2 miles total; paved, gravel, and natural surfaces* |
| OTHER USAGE | *Pedestrians only on forest trails* |
| STEEPNESS | *Level to gentle* |
| CONNECTING TRAILS | *None* |
| PARK SERVICES | *Restrooms, picnic shelters, community center, tennis courts, swimming pools, playing fields, fitness course* |
| DISABLED ACCESS | *Restrooms, buildings, pool* |

THE BEAUTY OF TITLOW HIDES BEHIND THE BUSY FAÇADE OF SWIMMING pool, playing fields, buildings, and two lagoons, one fresh, one tidal. To leave the high concentration of people, dogs, and ducks, walk past the activities areas, heading north on the gravel trail that parallels the Burlington Northern tracks. Suddenly the crowds dissipate and you walk in the shade of alders and graceful madronas. A fitness course winds its way over stream and wetlands through the forest.

At the maintenance road, turn left toward the beach. Here, in a secluded strip of forest above the sand, you'll find picnic tables and viewpoints over the water. To explore the beach, follow the old

**Water-smoothed pieces of driftwood make life-sized building logs**

boat launch ramp down. At low tide you have a half mile of sand and crabs, clams and seaweed to explore before reaching the southern end of Titlow.

Separated from the rest of the park by the railroad tracks, the southwestern corner features views, picnicking, and beachcombing. High on the old ferry dock pilings, wooden birdhouses await nesting martins. Interpretive signs tell about the tidal zones and the creatures living there. This is a favorite point for scuba divers and kayakers, so there's always lots of activity to watch. At high tide, you can walk the quarter-mile access road between the tracks and the beach for fine views of the water and the Tacoma Narrows Bridge.

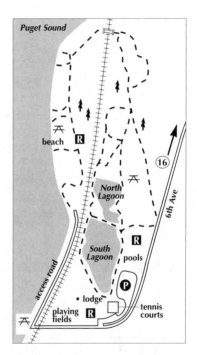

*How to Get There:* **From I-5 in Tacoma, take exit 132 (SR 16 west, Gig Harbor, Bremerton). Go about 4.5 miles and take the Jackson Ave exit. Turn left (south) on Jackson Ave. Go one block and turn right on 6th Ave which ends at the park. Metropolitan Park District of Tacoma (206) 305-1000.**

# #84
# WAPATO PARK

TACOMA, 6.5 MILES SOUTH OF DOWNTOWN

| | |
|---|---|
| HIGHLIGHTS | *Lake, wetlands, garden* |
| TRAIL | *1.4 miles total; paved and natural surfaces* |
| OTHER USAGE | *Bicycles* |
| STEEPNESS | *Level to gentle* |
| CONNECTING TRAILS | *None* |
| PARK SERVICES | *Restrooms, picnic shelters, playground, fishing pier, playing fields. Swimming beach, concessions, and paddle boats in summer only* |
| DISABLED ACCESS | *Restrooms, paved trail along lake, picnic area* |

FORMAL GARDENS AND A WHITE-TRELLISED PERGOLA WELCOME YOU TO this 30-acre lake set in an 80-acre park in suburban Tacoma. Away from the picnic areas and playing fields, you can find sanctuaries of marshland and mature forest.

Turn right at the garden entrance to the northern parking lot. Walk the paved road north over an old 1933 WPA-project bridge. To the right, in the forest, follow footpaths to the two-thirds-of-a-mile fitness course, or continue on the road, cutting left toward the marshland. A high footbridge lifts you over the cattails where red-winged blackbirds nest. Marsh wrens call *tsuck, tsuck* and flit from bush to bush. On the western side of the lake, join the paved trail that borders the water until it ends at private homes.

Return over the dike structure, where kids can fish year-round and from which you can watch the bottoms-up antics of the coots and mallards feeding among the water lilies. From the parking area, walk south under hundred-year-old fir and hemlock, past the swimming area and summer concessions. Footpaths connect the open lawns, playing fields, southern picnic area, and parking lot. Look for the old wrought iron lightpost slowly being absorbed by the dense bark of a Douglas fir. The park derives its name from *wapato*, a previously abundant aquatic root the Native Americans harvested from the lake.

***How to Get There:*** From I-5 in Tacoma, north- or southbound, take exit 129 (S 72nd St). Go east (right if northbound, left if southbound) on S 72nd St. Go 2 blocks and turn left (north) on S Sheridan St. Entrance is on the left at S Sheridan St and S 68th St. Summer entrance fee may apply. Metropolitan Park District of Tacoma (206) 305-1000.

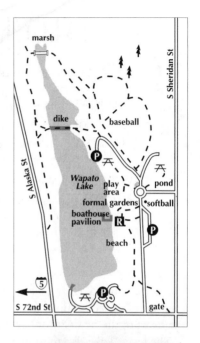

View across the marsh to Wapato Lake in summer

# #85
# SEELEY LAKE PARK

### LAKEWOOD, 8 MILES SOUTH OF TACOMA

| | |
|---|---|
| HIGHLIGHTS | *Young forest, wetlands* |
| TRAIL | *1.3-mile loop; graveled surface* |
| OTHER USAGE | *Pedestrians only* |
| STEEPNESS | *Gentle* |
| CONNECTING TRAILS | *None* |
| PARK SERVICES | *Restrooms, picnic area, community center, classes, sports courts* |
| DISABLED ACCESS | *Restrooms, community center* |

WRAPPING LIKE A CLOAK AROUND THE HIDDEN LAKE, THIS 1.3-MILE trail serves the community as a training walk or as a lunchtime stroll in the heart of the new City of Lakewood.

The term "Lake" is a misnomer, for Seeley Lake is a runoff catchment for the city, thus its water level fluctuates noticeably with the rainfall.

**Yum! Lunch is just beneath the surface for a dabbling mallard**

Despite this, the walk is a pleasant stroll on a wide, well-maintained path that provides green seclusion and, except for the eastern edge that parallels Lakewood Drive, some degree of silence. Young red alder saplings rustle in the breeze, and in the growing season white snowberries and red and black blackberries create a thicket of color and texture. Small marshes appear suddenly amidst the brush. In winter, with the thinning of the leaves, more of the pond is visible, and migrating waterfowl find much needed rest here on their long flights.

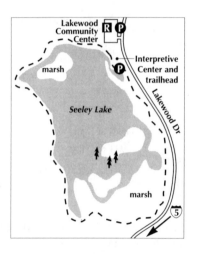

*How to Get There:* **From I-5 south of Tacoma, north- or southbound, take exit 125 (Lakewood). Turn north (left if northbound, right if southbound) onto Bridgeport Way. Go about 1 mile and turn right on Lakewood Dr SW. In 0.7 mile look for the Lakewood Community Center on the left. Trail parking is to the left of the Center. The Community Center is open daily until 11 PM with handicapped-accessible restrooms. Pierce County Parks (206) 593-4176.**

Choose Walks with Variety: *Avoid long, straight trails when walking with children unless they want to try out their tricycle while you walk. Playgrounds make good bribes for the end of a trail well walked. Streams are fun, but not if they're protected for salmon and can't be touched.*

# #86
# CHAMBERS CREEK TRAIL

### STEILACOOM, 12 MILES SOUTHWEST OF TACOMA

| | |
|---|---|
| HIGHLIGHTS | *Mature mixed forest, stream, estuary* |
| TRAIL | *1.5 miles one way; natural surface* |
| OTHER USAGE | *Pedestrians only* |
| STEEPNESS | *Steep* |
| CONNECTING TRAILS | *None* |
| PARK SERVICES | *None* |
| DISABLED ACCESS | *None* |

HIKE HIGH ON A WILDLAND HILLSIDE OF MOSS-COVERED BIGLEAF maples and Douglas firs you can hardly fit your arms around. Look out into the canopy of trees and down to the shimmering glimpse of Chambers Creek. Listen to the silence of the forest, broken by the song of a thrush or the rustling of a squirrel in the brush.

An unpretentious beginning leads to this well-traveled trail in a mature forest, just minutes from the I-5 corridor south of Tacoma. In summer, take a moment to walk to the bridge over Chambers Bay before starting up the trail; the forest is so dense with summer greenery that this may be your only chance to see the estuary, which resounds with the calls of the killdeer and shrills of the gulls. In winter, the bigleaf maples drop their screening leaves and allow views from the trail to the stream

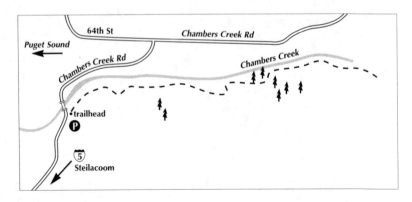

and estuary below. This trail is rough and steep. It's not advisable in wet weather, but when it's dry you can follow it to the top, where houses announce the end of parkland. Along this steep climb up the shoulder of the creek ravine, listen for the forest birds and the chattering squirrels.

A great blue heron motionless at the edge of an estuary

Pause at the spacious glen where the hillside is carved into an amphitheater of fern and salal.

Several side trails drop down toward the stream. The first leads to a clearing by the bay, the second to a high viewpoint over clear, rushing Chambers Creek. Old stumps make homes for owls and provide food for flickers and sapsuckers.

*How to Get There:* From I-5 south of Tacoma, northbound, take exit 119 (Dupont, Steilacoom) and head north on the Dupont-Steilacoom Hwy (which becomes Union Ave after leaving Ft Lewis, and in Steilacoom becomes Lafayette St then Chambers Creek Rd). Follow Chambers Creek Rd to just before it crosses Chambers Bay. Look on the right for a pullout (limited parking) and a signposted footpath into the forest.

From I-5 in Tacoma, southbound, take exit 129 (S 72nd St). Go west (right) on 74th St (which becomes Custer Dr in 2.3 miles). Go another 1.2 miles and turn right onto Steilacoom Blvd. Follow it into the town of Steilacoom. Turn right on Main St, then right again onto Lafayette St and proceed as above. Pierce County Parks (206) 593-4176.

# #87
# FORT STEILACOOM PARK

### 11 MILES SOUTHWEST OF TACOMA

| | |
|---|---|
| HIGHLIGHTS | *Lake, meadows, Rainier and Olympic views, historical site, bird-watching* |
| TRAIL | *7 miles total: 1-mile loop, paved; others, natural surface* |
| OTHER USAGE | *Bicycles, horses* |
| STEEPNESS | *Level to moderate* |
| CONNECTING TRAILS | *None* |
| PARK SERVICES | *Restrooms, picnic areas, playing fields, playground* |
| DISABLED ACCESS | *Picnic area, Waughop Lake trail* |

FROM FORT TO MENTAL HOSPITAL TO COUNTY PARK, THESE GROUNDS represent a chronicle of Washington history. Parade grounds from the 1850s have given way to meadow grasses, and old buildings have succumbed to the weight of time. There was never a stockade at Fort Steilacoom, which protected the settlers at the bustling Steilacoom port from 1849 to 1868. When soldiers left it became a mental hospital.

Today, as you walk these spacious meadows, you can see the old hospital cemetery grounds, dating from 1876 to 1953, and the restored 1930s farm buildings and barns.

From the southwestern corner of the parking area, near the barns, head west toward Waughop Lake. A wheelchair-accessible, 1-mile trail circumnavigates the very green lake under the shade of elms and redwoods. Willows gracefully dip their branches to the water, and mallards paddle about.

Climb the knoll on well-worn footpaths, past several old or-

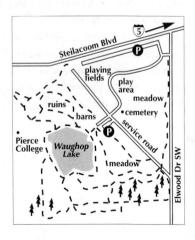

The still waters of Waughop Lake teem with aquatic life

chards and lines of poplars. At the top, you'll find the imposing ruins of the 1940s patients' ward, now used as a site to train emergency personnel in earthquake or bombing preparedness. Views here expand west to the Olympics and to Fox, McNeil, and Anderson Islands in the Tacoma Narrows. To the east Mount Rainier looms, and below you see Waughop Lake and the Pierce College campus.

Other trails weave like a spider's web through the meadows up to the southern forest boundary. Though you have 360 acres to explore, you're not likely to get lost: there's plenty of long-distance visibility across the meadows and from the hillocks.

*How to Get There:* From I-5 south of Tacoma, northbound, take exit 125 (Lakewood). Turn left onto Bridgeport Way. Go north on Bridgeport Way, crossing 100th St SW and Gravelly Lake Dr. Turn left on Steilacoom Blvd. Go about 1.5 miles and turn left onto Elwood Dr (across from 87th Ave SW). Turn right immediately on Dresden Lane into the park.

From I-5 in Tacoma, southbound, take exit 129 (S 72nd St). Go west (right) on 74th St which becomes Custer Drive in 2.3 miles (after crossing Lakewood Drive). Go another 1.2 miles and turn right on Steilacoom Blvd and proceed as above. Pierce County Parks (206) 593-4176.

# #88
# SPANAWAY PARK

### SPANAWAY, 15 MILES SOUTH OF TACOMA

| | |
|---|---|
| HIGHLIGHTS | *Lake, stream, wetlands* |
| TRAIL | *3 miles total; paved, gravel, and natural surfaces* |
| OTHER USAGE | *Bicycles on designated trails* |
| STEEPNESS | *Level to gentle* |
| CONNECTING TRAILS | *None* |
| PARK SERVICES | *Restrooms, picnic shelters, playground, fishing, playing fields, boat launch, swimming beach, Sprinkler Recreation Center* |
| DISABLED ACCESS | *Restrooms, picnic shelters, playground, fishing, playing fields, boat launch, beach* |

FOLLOW A WIDE, GRAVELED TRAIL ALONG THE EDGE OF THIS EXPANSIVE lake, or explore shaded trails through a wetland or forest—all just minutes from downtown Tacoma.

Like a mink changing color for the winter, this park, too, changes with the seasons. In summer the manicured lawns resound with the sound of families and children playing, motorboats, and jet-skis on the lake. The snack bar attracts crowds, and the aromas of ketchup and grilling supper fill the air. You can walk here then, but sometimes it's an effort: it's easy to rely on the car to move from one end of the long park to the other. Off-season, though, the park regains a more natural feel.

Fishermen cast their lines in hope of bass or trout. Migrant waterfowl glide on the still waters, and you can stroll the waterfront trail, then return by the upper playing fields, beneath majestic Douglas firs.

To the north, where the lake empties to a stream, two footbridges lead into a more sylvan setting of alders and willows, salal and ferns. The dirt trail is narrow, with exposed roots and rocks, climbing a gentle hill and then dropping to a wetland. The park boundary fence, the stream, and Old Military Road ensure that you can't get lost. Follow a stone-lined, narrow footpath along the edge of the wetland, and then return over the footbridges.

Across Old Military Road explore the many miles of informal forested trail that begin near Sprinker Recreation Center.

*How to Get There:* From I-5 south of Tacoma, north- or southbound, take exit 127 (SR 512 east, Puyallup). Go east for 2 miles on SR 512 and turn right (south) on SR 7 (Pacific Ave). Go 4.8 miles and turn right on Old Military Rd (152nd St E). Go 0.5 mile to the main gate. Sprinker Recreation Center and forest trails are on the right (north) side; the lake is on the left. Pierce County Parks (206) 593-4176.

Flocks of fluffy goslings are carefully herded by parent geese

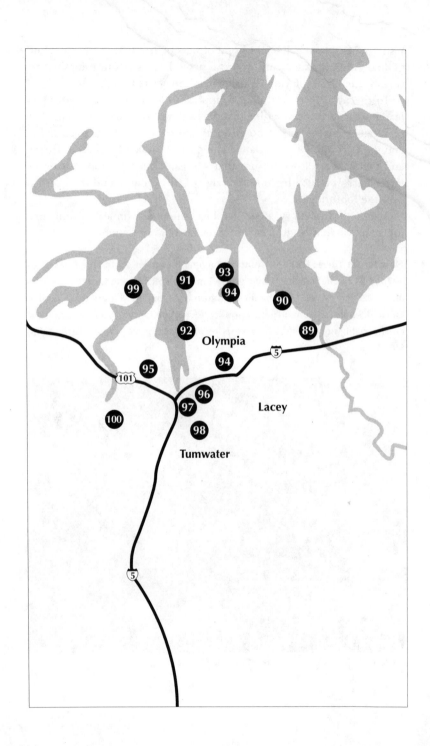

# IN AND AROUND OLYMPIA

# #89
# NISQUALLY NATIONAL WILDLIFE REFUGE

## On Puget Sound, 9.5 miles northeast of Olympia, 18 miles southwest of Tacoma

| | |
|---|---|
| HIGHLIGHTS | *Estuary, Olympic views, bird-watching* |
| TRAIL | *5-mile and 1-mile loops; gravel and natural surfaces* |
| OTHER USAGE | *Pedestrians only; no pets* |
| STEEPNESS | *Level* |
| CONNECTING TRAILS | *None* |
| PARK SERVICES | *Restrooms, viewing blinds, observation decks, education center* |
| DISABLED ACCESS | *Restrooms, interpretive area* |

COMPLETING ITS JOURNEY FROM THE HEIGHTS OF MOUNT RAINIER, the Nisqually River releases its pent-up energy into the broad expanse of the estuary. The air is rich with the scent of salt from the Sound and fresh water from the river. The open meadows and wetlands are vast, inviting exploration. High on the dike, you can wander between the berries and the brush where wrens and sparrows call and feed. Snow geese and white-fronted geese huddle into the receding tide line. Dozens of great blue herons stand like sentries of the wetland below, some intent on the fish that dart between their stiltlike legs, others staring as though trying to comprehend the human forms with binocular eyes. Green-belted kingfishers hover above their prey, while over the grasslands immature bald eagles practice soaring and diving.

Most visitors to the Refuge come for the birds: there are more than 100 species of resident waterfowl, raptors, and songbirds as well as over 20,000 migratory birds that gather here during fall and winter. Out on the dike, viewing blinds and platforms increase the chances of spotting and photographing wildlife.

But for people just interested in stretching their muscles, the level, 5-mile Brown Farm Dike Trail offers some of the finest walking in the region. Leaving the parking lot, you pass through the aromatic remains of the old orchard, where unpicked fruit hangs heavy on the bough in the fall. Dense planting around the old farmhouse (now an office) offers refuge to robins, sparrows, finches, and a chorus of other songbirds.

*How to Get There:* From I-5 between Tacoma and Olympia, north- or south-bound, take exit 114 (Nisqually). Turn west (left if northbound, right if south-bound) at the end of the ramp, and go under the freeway. Turn right (following signs) to the refuge. $2 admission fee, except holders of Golden Age and Golden Eagle Passes. Part of the Dike Trail loop is closed October 12 to January 12 each year because of hunting. National Wildlife Refuge (360) 753-9467.

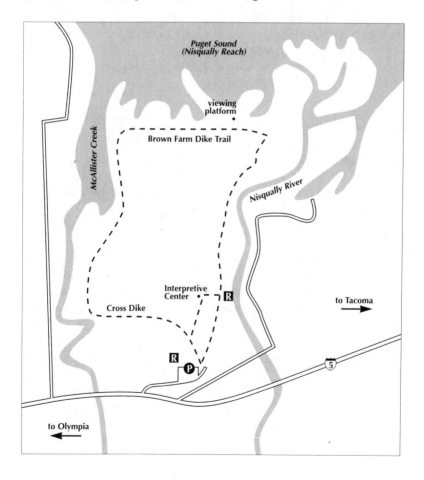

# #90
# TOLMIE STATE PARK

### On Puget Sound, 11 miles northeast of Olympia

| | |
|---|---|
| HIGHLIGHTS | *Saltwater beach, salt marsh, forest, Olympic views, bird-watching* |
| TRAIL | *4.3 miles; paved and natural surfaces* |
| OTHER USAGE | *Pedestrians only in forest; bicycles on paved trails* |
| STEEPNESS | *Level (beach) to steep* |
| CONNECTING TRAILS | *None* |
| PARK SERVICES | *Restrooms, picnic shelters, underwater park* |
| DISABLED ACCESS | *Restrooms, picnic area, edge of marsh* |

JELLYFISH, SCULPIN, AND ROCK CRABS SHARE THE SALTWATER MARSH with eelgrass and pickleweed. On the tidal flats young geoducks have been planted in plastic tubes to protect them from crabs and seagulls until they are a year old. Divers head offshore to explore the sunken barges that have created an underwater reef. You can explore the beach or head inland for miles of forest walking.

Start at the upper parking lot for a view of the Olympic Mountains across the Sound. A steep trail with railroad-tie steps leads to the beach and the lower picnic areas. As at other recreational beaches on the Sound, the best time for quiet and solitude is any day but a hot sunny one. If the tide is in, you can stop on the footbridge over the marsh for a view of the inhabitants. Offshore the usual waterfowl gather—more during fall and winter migration than in summer.

From the beach, a long loop trail takes you into the forest of lichen-covered trees. Boardwalks keep your feet dry while letting you examine the plant life along the way. Benches make good snack stops or resting points. A shortcut about halfway brings you back to the parking lot.

The park honors Dr. William Fraser Tolmie, a pioneer physician with the Hudson's Bay Company who served for 18 years at Fort Nisqually, just east of the present-day park. Married to a daughter of Chief Factor,

Children relish the cool muddy sand of Puget Sound beaches

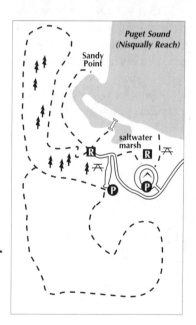

Tolmie was instrumental in returning peace to the region after the Indian Wars of 1855–56.

*How to Get There:* From I-5 between Olympia and Tacoma, north- or southbound, take exit 111 (SR 510, Yelm, Marvin Rd) and head west (left if northbound, right if southbound) on Marvin Rd NE. Go about 3.5 miles and turn right on 56th Ave NE. Go 0.4 mile to Hill Rd NE and turn left, then left again on 61st Ave NE to the park. The park is closed Mondays and Tuesdays from October 1 to March 31. Washington State Parks (800) 233-0321.

# #91
# BURFOOT PARK

### On Budd Inlet, 6 miles north of Olympia

| | |
|---|---|
| HIGHLIGHTS | *Saltwater beach, forest* |
| TRAIL | *2.6 miles total; natural surface* |
| OTHER USAGE | *Pedestrians only* |
| STEEPNESS | *Moderate to steep* |
| CONNECTING TRAILS | *None* |
| PARK SERVICES | *Restrooms, playground, interpretive trail, picnic shelters* |
| DISABLED ACCESS | *Restrooms, "Meadow Shelter," picnic area* |

MOST OF THE WONDER OF BURFOOT PARK IS HIDDEN FROM THE CASUAL first-time visitor. The central lawn/picnic area is so large and appealing that you might believe it's all there is to the park. But drive or walk the parking loop, and you'll discover the three trail entrances into the cool enchantment of the forest, which descends to the beach on Budd Inlet.

For an easy stroll, start on the Horizon Trail nature loop, which documents the changes in the forest since it was logged in the 1890s. Moisture encourages moss and old man's beard to grow prolifically, and they cover the trees with a thick green shawl.

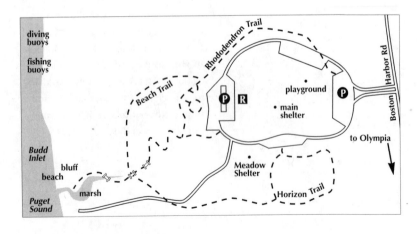

**Lush undergrowth borders the trail at Burfoot Park**

Along the Rhododendron Trail a right fork descends the ridge of a ravine carpeted with sword fern. Here the wrens call and hop on downed logs, their short perky tails bobbing.

A clear *rat-a-tat-tat* may sound from above. High on a snag, pileated woodpeckers with iridescent red crests may be circling the tree, probing the bark for grubs. Farther along the fern-bedecked ravine, more snags bear the characteristic rectangular holes made by these birds, the largest western woodpeckers.

Though there are several trails, there is no need for signs: all trails lead to the beach. At low tide crows stride the beach, and great blue herons may be feeding on small fish in the shallows. To the south, the dome of the State Capitol rises between forested hills.

*How to Get There:* From I-5 in Olympia, northbound, take exit 105 (City Center, Port of Olympia). Stay hard right following Port of Olympia signs. At the end of the ramp, take a right and go under the freeway. Go straight onto Plum St (which becomes East Bay Dr then Boston Harbor Dr). Go 6 miles and look for the park on the left.

From I-5 in Olympia, southbound, take exit 105B. Follow signs for Port of Olympia, staying right toward Plum St. Follow Plum St north and proceed as above. Thurston County Parks (360) 786-5595.

# #92
# PRIEST POINT PARK

OLYMPIA, 2.5 MILES NORTH OF DOWNTOWN

|  |  |
|---|---|
| HIGHLIGHTS | *Forest, saltwater beach, estuary, art* |
| TRAIL | *6 miles roundtrip; natural surface* |
| OTHER USAGE | *Pedestrians only* |
| STEEPNESS | *Gentle to moderate* |
| CONNECTING TRAILS | *None* |
| PARK SERVICES | *Restrooms, picnic shelters, wading pool, basketball hoops* |
| DISABLED ACCESS | *Restrooms, picnic areas* |

WARM SUN FILTERS THROUGH THE SUMMER CANOPY OF BIGLEAF MAPLES and Douglas firs. The air feels cool and then warm, and is fragrant with the delicious, almost imperceptible scent of blackberry blossoms. Ellis Cove Trail, the primary walking trail of Priest Point Park, meanders for 3 miles through woodland magic, passing creeks and ravines and then

**Wood-chip paths and bridges on Ellis Cove Trail**

traversing bluffs above southern Puget Sound. Sword ferns, huckleberry, and salal weave a lush green carpet beneath towering western red cedars. This forest so well cocoons you in a sylvan spell that it's hard to believe urban Olympia lies just minutes away.

The wide, soft, wood-chip path is easy on the feet, and quiet: bicycles and horses are prohibited. The sculptured wooden trail signs are imaginative and playful. At one junction a carved squirrel shows the way out, and elsewhere a sea otter perches on the trail post. Look for the unexpected sculpture of the small black bear climbing a trunk high above the trail.

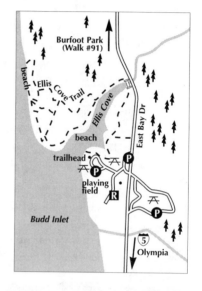

Although you must retrace the trail to return to the parking lot, there are several internal loops to explore. No fear of getting lost, what with all the wooden animals to give directions. Sturdy wooden bridges lead you down into the cool ravine where Ellis Creek ends in a tidal estuary.

Interpretive signs explain the life of the estuary and the native peoples who traveled to this point on Budd Inlet to trade. A French missionary lived here from 1848 to 1860. After he left, the virgin forest was reduced to stumps within 40 years. In 1905 the City of Olympia bought Priest Point Park, and 75 years later created Ellis Cove Trail. This is one trail to savor, over and over again.

***How to Get There:*** **From I-5 in Olympia, northbound, take exit 105 (City Center, Port of Olympia). Stay hard right following Port of Olympia signs. At the end of the ramp, take a right and go under the freeway. Go straight onto Plum St (which becomes East Bay Dr then Boston Harbor Dr). The park is about 2 miles north of town, with the entrance on the right. Enter the park and pass over Boston Harbor Dr following signs to the Ellis Cove Trail.**

**From I-5 in Olympia, southbound, take exit 105B. Follow signs for Port of Olympia, staying right toward Plum St. Follow Plum St north and proceed as above. Olympia Parks (360) 753-8380.**

# #93
# WOODARD BAY PRESERVE

## ON WOODARD BAY, 5 MILES NORTH OF OLYMPIA

| | |
|---|---|
| HIGHLIGHTS | *Nature preserve, seals, forest, estuary, bird-watching* |
| TRAIL | *0.5 mile one way, paved; 1.75 miles one way, natural surface* |
| OTHER USAGE | *Pedestrians only; no pets* |
| STEEPNESS | *Level* |
| CONNECTING TRAILS | *Chehalis Western Trail (Walk #94), via bridge on country road* |
| PARK SERVICES | *Nature classes; kayak launch (April through August only)* |
| DISABLED ACCESS | *Paved path to bay* |

BEGINNING AT THE PAVED ENTRANCE ROAD, STROLL THE HALF MILE through moss-draped second-growth forest to Henderson Inlet. You may hear the sharp hammering of woodpeckers or the hoarse, barking sound of the green-backed heron. If the breeze is right, you'll smell the

Licorice ferns spring from moss-covered trees in Woodard Bay Preserve

salt water before you see it. The state of the tide determines whether you see shimmering, wet mud or hear the lapping of wavelets on the shore. The clearing at this tip of land was once a bustling log dump where timber was transferred from railroad cars to the water, to be floated to mills in Everett.

The logging sounds are gone now, giving way to the persistent chatter of belted kingfishers as they hover, searching for lunch below. Soon you hear the yarps and groans of harbor seals, 300 to 400 of them. In this maternity colony females and their pups rest on the log booms or sun themselves on the shores. They are easily stressed, so enjoy them from afar. With binoculars you can watch the cormorants and gulls standing like nursemaids on old pilings above sleeping seals.

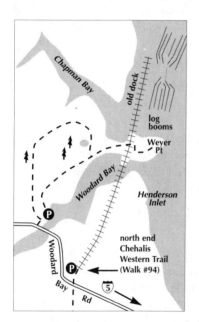

For variety, take the forest loop back to the entrance. This natural path ranges up and down gentle hillocks and through forest wetlands over wooden boardwalks. Overhead stand massive maples with spreading branches that could hold swings for giants. Sturdy cedars and hemlocks embrace their nurse logs, or form their own colonies of two or three trunks growing together. When the trail parallels the shore of Chapman's Bay high on a ridge, you can look down on the flocks of shore birds or solitary great blue herons feeding.

*How to Get There:* **From I-5 north of Olympia, north- or southbound, take exit 108 (Sleater-Kinney Rd). Go north (left) on Sleater-Kinney Rd about 5 miles, until it takes a sharp turn to the left becoming 56th Ave NE. Go immediately right on Schinke Rd (which becomes Woodard Bay Rd and crosses the tip of Woodard Bay on a bridge). Park immediately on the right in front of the gates to the authorities–only entrance road. Woodard Bay is closed to kayakers from Labor Day to April 1 because of the extreme sensitivity of waterfowl. Department of Natural Resources (360) 748-2383.**

# #94
# CHEHALIS WESTERN TRAIL

OLYMPIA (2.5 MILES NORTH OF DOWNTOWN) NORTH TO WOODARD BAY
(5 MILES NORTH OF OLYMPIA)

| | |
|---|---|
| HIGHLIGHTS | *Ponds, pastures, forest, wetlands* |
| TRAIL | *6 miles one way; southern end paved, northern end gravel* |
| OTHER USAGE | *Bicycles, horses on designated sections* |
| STEEPNESS | *Level* |
| CONNECTING TRAILS | *Woodard Bay Preserve (Walk #93), via bridge on Woodward Bay Road; no bicycles* |
| PARK SERVICES | *Benches* |
| DISABLED ACCESS | *Paved trail at southern end* |

STEP FROM SHOPPING-CENTER MADNESS INTO WOODS AND WETLANDS where the sweet chirping of crickets replaces the gunning of engines. This newly converted rails-to-trails thoroughfare offers fast-paced walking or quiet contemplation of the plants and pastures framing it.

At the southern end, the path runs between homes and apartments for part of a mile, then alternates woods with pasture. North of 26th Avenue, a pastoral feeling prevails. Horses come to the fence to greet you, and raptors may be soaring over the meadows in search of mice. Small ponds and wetlands add more tranquil greenery.

For 56 years this passage from Olympia to Woodard Bay was owned and operated by the Weyerhaeuser Timber Company to move logs from cutting sites to the transshipment site on Woodard Bay. When Washington State acquired the Woodard Bay land in the mid-1980s, Weyerhaeuser threw the rail trail into the deal and pulled the track and ties.

At the northern end, the trail begins south of the tidal flats of Woodard Bay, crosses under the road, then runs in a straight line as far as you can see. The woods are older here, and denser, but then they open to farmland. Halfway, near Shincke Road, a large marsh-rimmed pond hosts the usual colorful assortment: kingfishers, red-winged black-

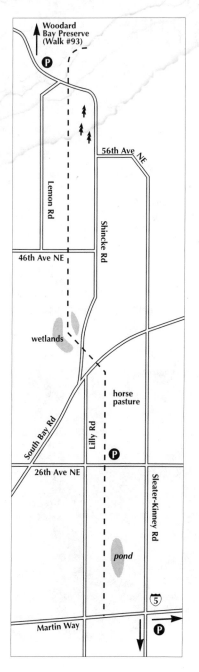

birds, marsh wrens, and great blue herons.

As on other rails-to-trails journeys, be prepared for street crossings: keep kids close, especially if they're on bikes or blades.

*How to Get There:* To reach the northern end: follow directions for Woodard Bay Preserve (Walk #93). Parking is on the right before the bridge over the bay.

To reach the southern end: From I-5 north of Olympia, northbound, take exit 108B (Sleater-Kinney Rd). Southbound, take exit 108 (Sleater-Kinney Rd). Go north on Sleater-Kinney Rd. Take the first left onto Martin Way. Immediately look on your right for the paved trail, a sign, and a graveled parking lot. The only designated parking is back a block at K-Mart. The store has given permission for trail users to park in the western-most spaces. (Stroller or wheelchair users may want to be dropped at the trail.)

Alternatively, you can access the trail by continuing north on Sleater-Kinney Rd about 1.5 miles, and turning left on 26th Ave NE. Park by the road where the trail crosses. Department of Natural Resources (360) 748-2383.

# #95
# YAUGER PARK

**OLYMPIA, 1.5 MILES WEST OF DOWNTOWN**

| | |
|---|---|
| HIGHLIGHTS | *Young forest, demonstration garden* |
| TRAIL | *2 miles total; natural surface* |
| OTHER USAGE | *Pedestrians only* |
| STEEPNESS | *Level* |
| CONNECTING TRAILS | *None* |
| PARK SERVICES | *Restrooms, picnic shelter, playground, playing fields, horseshoe pits, classes* |
| DISABLED ACCESS | *Restrooms* |

THIS NEIGHBORHOOD PARK NEAR OLYMPIA'S APARTMENTS AND SHOPPING malls offers green respite in the form of a three-quarter-mile jogging trail (also great for walking) and a nature trail through a young red alder and maple forest.

**Red alder leaves against a clear sky**

For the longest walk, park at the southern end of the park, and stroll the greenway between playing fields and the Apple Creek Apartments. Past the playground, the jogging trail heads east around the sports fields, but just beyond that a trail sign leads you into the young forest. This winding, level trail was built by students from Capitol High School in 1986. They cleared the trail, built the platforms and boardwalks, and created the map at the trailhead.

The trail makes two small loops through this forest of saplings. Look in the branches for American robins, rufous-sided towhees, or dark-eyed juncos. In summer, American goldfinches often alight on the slender branches. The trail crosses a seasonal stream and pauses at viewing platforms, where you can bird-watch or just relax under the open sky. Enjoy the cool of the grove of western red cedar with its lichen-covered stumps.

After reaching the end, return to the trailhead, then turn right on the gravel maintenance road. Behind a fence is "Dirt Works," a city demonstration garden with lilies, a Shakespearean herb garden, groundcovers, worm bins, and information signs.

*How to Get There:* **From I-5 in Olympia, north- or southbound, take exit 104 (US 101, Aberdeen). Head north on US 101 and take the Black Lake Blvd SW exit. Turn right on Black Lake Blvd SW then left at the next light on Cooper Point Rd W. Turn left onto Capital Mall Dr. Yauger Park is immediately on the right. Open until 10 PM. "Dirt Works" is open Saturdays and some weekdays May through September (360) 786-5441. Olympia Parks (360) 753-8380.**

# #96
# OLYMPIA WATERSHED PARK

### OLYMPIA, 1 MILE SOUTH OF DOWNTOWN

| | |
|---|---|
| HIGHLIGHTS | *Forested basin, wetlands, salmon-spawning creek, bird-watching* |
| TRAIL | *1.5-mile loop; natural surface* |
| OTHER USAGE | *Pedestrians only (no jogging)* |
| STEEPNESS | *Moderate to steep* |
| CONNECTING TRAILS | *None* |
| PARK SERVICES | *None* |
| DISABLED ACCESS | *None* |

THIS GREEN AND MOSSY BASIN, JUST MINUTES FROM DOWNTOWN Olympia, encircles you with a rich scent of wetland forest and the soothing sounds of birds and water. Bracken, horsetail, maples, and alder line the natural pathway that stretches from the rim to the streambed and

**Boardwalk trails safeguard the wetlands at Olympia Watershed Park**

back. Trees tumbled by winter's windstorms lie like giant matchsticks, their roots exposed like pinwheels.

From the parking lot, descend into the forest, taking the loop in either direction. Steps lead down to marshes where green algae creates an Impressionist painting on the water's surface. Sword ferns, bracken, and maidenhair ferns line the trail. In this deep, shady forest of Douglas fir, and bigleaf maple and alder, be ready for banana slugs and skunk cabbage, natural inhabitants of so wet and lush a place.

**Pack It In, Pack It Out:** *Many parks and most natural-surface trails have no trash collection. Carry a plastic bag in your pocket or your day pack for trash.*

This is a popular walk, despite its ruggedness—or perhaps because of it. Young families come with children in tow, teaching them the wonders of the streambed, where salmon spawn and tadpoles scoot about like tiny bumper cars gone crazy. Dogs are welcome, but only on leash, to protect the fragile habitat and sensitive replanting areas. Boardwalks, too, protect the wetlands and help you keep your feet dry; sturdy wooden bridges offer vantage points above clear, sandybottomed Moxlie Creek.

*How to Get There:* **From I-5 in Olympia, northbound, take exit 105 (City Center, Port of Olympia). Stay hard right following Port of Olympia signs. At the end of the ramp, turn left (which is Henderson Blvd, but not marked) and go 0.25 mile to the trailhead on the left.**

**From I-5 in Olympia, southbound, take exit 105B. Follow signs for Port of Olympia, staying left for Henderson Blvd. Go under the freeway and look on the left in 0.25 mile for the trailhead. Olympia Parks (360) 753-8380.**

# 97

# HISTORICAL PARK AND CAPITOL LAKE

## TUMWATER (2 MILES SOUTH OF OLYMPIA) TO DOWNTOWN OLYMPIA

| | |
|---|---|
| HIGHLIGHTS | *Lake, wetlands, Mount Rainier views, art, salmon in Deschutes River, bird-watching* |
| TRAIL | *2 miles one way to end of Capitol Lake, with 0.8-mile loop; mostly paved* |
| OTHER USAGE | *Bicycles* |
| STEEPNESS | *Level* |
| CONNECTING TRAILS | *None* |
| PARK SERVICES | *Restrooms, playgrounds, picnic shelter, fishing docks* |
| DISABLED ACCESS | *Restrooms and trail (except loop trail east of Marathon Park and marsh trail in Historical Park)* |

NESTLED IN A POCKET OF MARSH AND GREENERY BENEATH THE RAMPARTS of I-5, tiny Historical Park may not be a long-distance destination in it-self, but after strolling its garden-like setting of wild roses and marsh walks, you can head north under the freeway to the shores of Capitol Lake and on to Marathon Park and Percival Landing for a longer walk.

Near the underpass by Histori-cal Park, a dock provides access to the lake and a close-up view of the reeds that adorn its edges. Blackbirds whistle *tse-er, tse-er* and great blue herons study the water for lunch. The trail continues around the southern edge of the

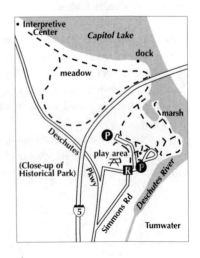

lake, through meadows and past the hives of honeybees established by local beekeepers in 1989. Despite its proximity to the freeway, this stretch of trail is surprisingly quiet except for the undulating song of robins and the chirps of wrens.

The lake was first proposed in 1911 as a means of trapping sediment from the Deschutes River but was not created until 1951. Today this lake is home to migrating and resident flocks of, among others, western grebes, red-winged blackbirds, juncos, pied-billed grebes, scaups, ruddy ducks, and swallows.

On reaching the Deschutes Parkway, the sidewalk trail borders the lake, with fine views of Mount Rainier and the Capitol buildings. For a northern loop, cut through Marathon Park, an oasis of lawn and cattails. Take the wooden bridge east to the gravel road that leads to Percival Landing. Complete the circle around the northern end, where the salt scent of Budd Inlet mixes with the freshwater air from the lake.

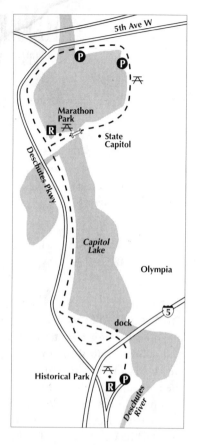

*How to Get to There:* Historical Park: From I-5 just south of Olympia, northbound, take exit 103 (Deschutes Way). Continue straight from the ramp through 1 stop sign, then turn right on Simmons Rd which leads into the park.

From I-5 just south of Olympia, southbound, take exit 103 (2nd Ave). At the flashing light turn left on Custer Way which crosses the freeway. Immediately at the end of the overpass, take a sharp right, curving down to a stop sign on Deschutes Way. Turn right on Deschutes Way, then right again onto Simmons Rd into the park. Tumwater Parks (360) 754-4160.

# #98
# PIONEER PARK
## (TUMWATER)

### TUMWATER, 4 MILES SOUTH OF OLYMPIA

| | |
|---|---|
| HIGHLIGHTS | *Meadow, river* |
| TRAIL LENGTH | *1.5 miles total; paved, gravel, and natural surfaces* |
| OTHER USAGE | *Bicycles* |
| STEEPNESS | *Level* |
| CONNECTING TRAILS | *None* |
| PARK SERVICES | *Restrooms, playing fields, playground* |
| DISABLED ACCESS | *Restrooms, paved trail* |

THIS SMALL NEIGHBORHOOD PARK WITH A RURAL FEEL AND OPEN meadows lies only minutes from downtown Olympia. Here you can walk well-defined trails through open grassland, or explore the banks of the Deschutes River. A new trail system, completed in 1996, has enlarged the park, and now it appeals not only to playground users and ball players but to lovers of gentle walks.

Nestled in a curve of the clear but shallow-running river, the meadow hosts rabbits and shrews, food for the hunting hawks overhead. From the parking lot, turn south from the playing fields and cross the natural meadow. The row of cottonwoods and alders defines the river bank, where you can wander the sandy edge or picnic on the graveled bar. No swimming is allowed, but you can stop and throw a fishing line. Back in the meadow, take a different loop to return to the cars. If it's a clear day, look for the white crown of Mount Rainier to the east.

Shallow river banks invite exploration

*How to Get There:* From I-5 south of Olympia, northbound, take exit 101 (Airdustrial Way). Turn right (east) on Airdustrial Way and follow it to the end (about 1 mile). Turn left on Henderson Blvd and go about 0.6 mile. The park is on the left just past the Deschutes River.

From I-5 just south of Olympia, southbound, take exit 103 (2nd Ave).

Safe Walks with Kids: *Establish clear rules for on-the-trail-behavior: Stay in sight, no running on forest paths, walk on the right side on multiuse trails, stand still to let horses pass, and always ask to pet horses or dogs. Know what you're touching, know what you're eating.*

At the flashing light, turn left on Custer Way which crosses the freeway. Continue on Custer Way through 1 light, then turn right at Cleveland Ave. Go 1.2 miles and turn right on Henderson Blvd. Go 0.5 mile, across Yelm Hwy and the railroad tracks. The park is on the right at the bottom of the hill. Tumwater Parks (360) 754-4160.

# #99
# FRYE COVE PARK

## On Eld Inlet, 12 miles northwest of Olympia

| | |
|---|---|
| HIGHLIGHTS | *Saltwater beach, forest* |
| TRAIL | *2 miles total; gravel and natural surfaces* |
| OTHER USAGE | *Pedestrians only* |
| STEEPNESS | *Level to gentle* |
| CONNECTING TRAILS | *None* |
| PARK SERVICES | *Restrooms, picnic area, shelters* |
| DISABLED ACCESS | *Restrooms, gravel trail from parking lot to picnic area* |

TUCKED AWAY ON ONE OF THE MYRIAD FINGER-INLETS OF SOUTHERN PUGET Sound, this forest and beach park entices with the twin luxuries of silence and seclusion.

Low tide at Frye Cove allows for longer walks along the shore

Entering the forest in summer, the bigleaf maples and alders shield you from the brilliance of the sun on the Sound. Licorice ferns adorn the moss on the maples like miniature Dr. Seuss characters on parade around the trunk. Catkins from the red alders dangle above the trail and speckle the path.

Last logged a hundred years ago, the forest has a mature presence, and the air carries the heady scent of cedar and salt. Hemlocks, some over 200 feet tall, drape their graceful branches above the trail. Benches and observation decks are placed for glimpses of the Sound and beach below and a raised walkway carries you over a dense ravine of sword ferns.

When you complete a loop at the parking lot, descend Cove Trail, at first gentle, then steep, to arrive at the southern end of the beach. Air holes of a million clams dapple the sand-and-mud beach at low tide, and palm-sized clams and oysters provide feasts for crows and gulls.

**Bring a Bucket and Shovel:** *Many Puget Sound beaches are open for clamming. Some are seasonally closed; others are permanently closed due to pollution. For information, call the individual park or the Red Tide Hotline, (800) 562-5632.*

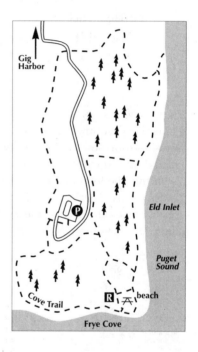

*How to Get There:* From I-5 in Olympia, north- or southbound, take exit 104 (US 101 north, Aberdeen). Stay on US 101 toward Shelton, and take the Steamboat Island Rd exit. Go north on Steamboat Island Rd NW about 5.8 miles and turn right on Young Rd NW. Go about 2 miles and turn left on 61st Ave NW into the park. Thurston County Parks (360) 786-5595.

# #100
# MCLANE CREEK NATURE TRAIL

**6 MILES SOUTHWEST OF OLYMPIA**

|  |  |
|---|---|
| HIGHLIGHTS | *Beaver ponds, wetlands, forest, salmon-spawning creek* |
| TRAIL | *1.1-mile loop; paved and natural surfaces* |
| OTHER USAGE | *Pedestrians only* |
| STEEPNESS | *Level to gentle* |
| CONNECTING TRAILS | *None* |
| PARK SERVICES | *Restrooms, interpretive signs* |
| DISABLED ACCESS | *Restrooms, trail* |

ENTER A FOREST IN HEALING, 60 YEARS AFTER LOGGERS TOOK OUT THE giants. Huge stumps show the scars of springboards but now serve as nurse logs for new saplings. Beavers maintain their ponds, and black-tailed deer and coyotes roam the open grassland at dawn and dusk.

Starting the loop to the left of the parking lot brings you first to the beaver ponds. These elusive but energetic rodents may not be easy to see, but you can observe the evidence of their work: freshly gnawed alders and cottonwoods lie tumbled along the water's edge. In winter

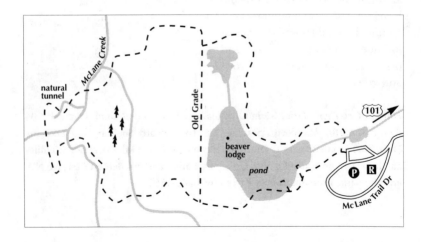

the pond is full, almost overflowing, and alive with ducks, geese, herons, frogs, otter, muskrats, and salamanders. Sometimes fall floods wash the dam out and the pond drains, but within six months the beavers can re-build and refill the pond.

A cutoff trail, the Old Grade, makes a shorter loop or can be ex-plored as a side trip from the main trail. This is a remnant of old log-ging days, when locomotives chugged through here on their way to the Mud Bay Timber Company on the Sound, just five miles away.

On the southern edge of the loop you walk in a forest of western red cedar and Douglas fir. Moss and lichen adorn the massive limbs, and woodpeckers leave their markings where they have bored for insects. Sparkling-clear McLane Creek is home to spawning salmon. Interpre-tive signs along the trail help you envision the creek and surround-ing habitat in all their seasonal changes.

*How to Get There:* **From I-5 in Olympia, north- or southbound, take exit 104 (US 101 north, Aberdeen). Take the Mud Bay/2nd Ave exit, turn left at the stop and go over the free-way. Take the first left onto McKenzie Rd (which becomes Delphi Rd). Go about 3 miles to the sign for McLane Creek Demonstration Forest and Nature Trail. Department of Natural Resources (360) 748-2383.**

**How Long Will It Take?** *The average adult walks at about 2–3 mph; children under age seven, about half that speed; bird-watchers— well, that depends. Variables include age and energy level, activities along the way, and trail conditions. Once you know your own pace and that of your friends or family, you'll know how long to allow for a 2-mile walk on gently hilly terrain.*

# INDEX OF WALKS AND PARKS

# INDEX OF WALK FEATURES
# AND ACTIVITIES

# REFERENCES

## PARKS AND RECREATION DEPARTMENTS

### City

Auburn (253) 931-3043
Bainbridge Island (206)
842-2306
Bellevue (425) 455-6881
Bothell (425) 486-3256
Des Moines (206) 870-6527
Edmonds (425) 771-0230
Everett (425) 257-8300
Issaquah (425) 391-1008
Kent (253) 859-3992
Kirkland (206) 828-1217
Lynnwood (206) 771-4030
Mercer Island (206) 236-3545
Mountlake Terrace (206)
776-9173
Olympia (360) 753-8380
Redmond (425) 556-2300
Renton (425) 235-2568
Seattle (206) 684-4075
Tacoma (253) 305-1000
Tukwila (206) 433-1843
Tumwater (360) 754-4160
Vashon Island (206) 463-9602

### County

King County (206) 296-4232
Pierce County (253) 593-4176
Snohomish County (425)
339-1208
Thurston County (360) 786-5595

### State

Department of Natural
Resources (800) 527-3305
Washington State Parks
Information Center
(800) 233-0321

## OTHER ADMINISTRATIONS

Bellevue Botanical Garden
(425) 451-3755
Center for Urban Horticulture
(206) 543-8616
Kubota Garden Foundation
(206) 725-5060
National Oceanic and
Atmospheric Administration
(NOAA) (206) 526-4548
Nisqually National Wildlife
Refuge (360) 753-9467
Port of Seattle (206) 728-3000
Washington Park Arboretum
(206) 543-8800

## ORGANIZATIONS

Regional Audubon Societies:
*(Local chapters that organize
naturalist-led walks through the
parks.)*

Black Hills Audubon
Society (Olympia area)
(360) 352-7299
East Lake Washington
Audubon Society (Bellevue
area) (425) 451-3717
Pilchuck Audubon Society
(Snohomish County and
Camano Island)
(425) 252-0926
Rainier Audubon Society
(South King County)
(253) 939-6411
Seattle Audubon Society
(206) 523-4483
Tahoma Audubon Society
(Pierce County)
(253) 565-9278

Evergreen State Volkssport Association (800) 828-WALK
*Sponsors noncompetitive walking events for all ages; 50 clubs throughout Washington.*

Issaquah Alps Trails Club Hotline (206) 328-0480
*Members explore Tiger, Cougar, and Squak Mountains and their volunteer work parties maintain and upgrade trails and habitat.*

Cascade and Sammamish Orienteering Clubs Hotline (206) 783-3866
*Clubs hold meets involving cross-country navigation by orienteers on foot around a preset course using a map and compass.*

Pacific Pacers (206) 524-4721
*Promotes race-walking as a fitness and competitive sport for all ages.*

The Mountaineers (206) 284-6310
*Members participate in a variety of recreational outdoor activities, including special youth, family, singles, and seniors events.*

Washington Trails Association (206) 625-1367
*The largest volunteer trail maintenance organization in the state, the WTA also produces Signpost, a monthly magazine featuring hiking destinations throughout the Pacific Northwest.*

## MAPS

For many of the parks included in the book, maps are available free of charge at the trailhead. The following maps can be purchased (fee as of press time):

**Map of Lord Hill Regional Park**
*Send $5 to:*
Philco Printing
221 SW 153rd St, Ste 265
Burien, WA 98166

**Mercer Island Trails Guide**
*Send $1 to:*
City of Mercer Island
9611 SE 36th St
Mercer Island, WA 98040

**Tiger Mountain Map**
(includes Tiger Mountain State Forest, Squak Mountain State Park, Cougar Mountain Regional Wildland Park, and Tradition Plateau)
*Send $2.50 to:*
Issaquah Chamber of Commerce
155 NW Gilman Blvd
Issaquah, WA 98027
*Also available for pick-up only at:*
Issaquah Parks and Recreation
301 Rainier Blvd S
Issaquah
(206) 391-1008